It's Not Personal.
It's Strictly Business:

The Godfather Way of
Surviving, Conniving and
Thriving in Corporate America

TONY SERRI

ISBN: 1439259658
ISBN-13: 9781439259658
Library of Congress Control Number: 2009910147

Dedication

Dedicated to my beautiful wife Babette, who believed in me when others asked her, "Why are you still with Tommy?" or said, "I know this guy who's a doctor. He's divorced. Besides, it won't be a date. It'll just be *coffee*."

This book, and, more importantly, any royalties are for you. You've earned every penny, all three of them, for being the best wife and friend to me and the greatest mom to our boys.

It's Not Personal. It's Strictly Business:
Table of Contents

Preface

WORKING IN A BIG CORPORATION CAN BE A STRUGGLE FOR SOME OF US. We feel anxious, bored, underappreciated or disconnected to the people we work with. Many people, in fact, are profoundly miserable in corporate America. For these people, calling work a "struggle" is a bit like calling the Crusades a "desert field trip." For them, work is a long, never-ending march of futility, hopelessness, and frustration; one that occasionally offers a dental and vision plan. If you find that you're approaching something close to a nervous breakdown every day by lunch, or find yourself looking at Army recruiting posters and wondering what might have been, or looking around your office at least once day and asking yourself, "How did I end up here?" then this book will help you.

The Godfather saga may seem like an odd place to get a business lifeline. After all, these were movies where the principles would decapitate a racehorse in lieu of writing a business letter, and where the heads of the various businesses spent a majority of their screen time trying to kill each other and lying about it. What does that have to do with the fact that you'd rather cut off your own thumbs than go to the company picnic?

But putting aside the mayhem and machine gun fire, these were movies about business, or, more precisely, about the true nature of people when money was involved. Business is a tough game, played by tough people. If you hate your boss for being dishonest or your co-workers for being backstabbers, you really shouldn't. They are playing business by the *right* rules. It's you who haven't been. You may be able to pat yourself on the back

Preface

for being a stand-up guy but the bottom line is that you are handicapping yourself. The unemployment office is filled with stand-up guys who are currently standing up in line, waiting for their state checks.

You're biggest mistake is that you are bringing integrity to the workplace, a place that has as much use these days for integrity as it does carbon paper or floppy disks. It's the same for teamwork or "positive change." These days, being a positive force for change at work will just get you steam-rolled. You can end up being your company's equivalent of the lone protester in Tiananmen Square, another stand-up guy. Nobody cares about "positive change" or "continuous improvement" anymore. Companies still pay it lip service, but those notions are so 2003. You need to play tough—dirty and political—as the Corleones did.

You're probably thinking, *that's not me. I can't do that.* If the idea of playing in the mud leaves a gritty aftertaste in your mouth, this book can show you how to rinse it out. The good news is that playing dirty in the workplace doesn't make you a bad person. Just a richer one. There are bad people who do bad things in the workplace, and there are good people who do bad things, but *only at work*. That's what you should shoot for (metaphorically). But even if you choose to be a good person, doing good things (not advisable), you'll benefit from knowing how to recognize the schemers, the manipulators, and the liars.

Here's a clue. It's everybody around you. You need to play their game, or at least understand how they think, or you'll get left behind. Doing bad things in the workplace doesn't make you a bad father, daughter, husband, or sister. It just means you're keeping up with everyone else. Was Marlon Brando a bad guy because he played Vito Corleone? Were Al Pacino and Lee Strasburg evil men because they played crime bosses? Hopefully, you said "No."

And that's where your head needs to be. Take away all the shooting, blackmailing, and threatening, and what the Corleones were really all about was playing dirty at work, while playing nice at home. Sure, they would strangle the occasional co-worker with a wire hanger or do some really bad things to animals. That's the kind of stuff *you* want to avoid. That stuff is wrong in every sense of the word. Fun to watch, sure, but impractical from today's business standpoint.

You can talk about positive forces in the workplace, you can even try to be one, but the reality is that it's the negative forces, or, more precisely, the people who aren't afraid to sell someone out, lie to their face, or intimidate others, that are making the big dough. And most of them are sleeping pretty well at night, in big, expensive houses. But if you could manage to play a little dirtier at work, while still feeling good about yourself, you might end up making a lot more money and actually sleeping better at night in your own big house.

This is a book that will hopefully open your eyes, or at least confirm what you already suspected about your workplace, using examples from the greatest screen saga ever filmed. In the end, it may not make you filthy rich, but I promise that after reading some of these chapters, the people at work will make a whole lot more sense to you.

Leave your guns, take your cannoli, and let's get started.

* * *

1. Fredo vs. Frodo

I OWE VITO CORLEONE MY LIFE. Maybe not quite "my life," but *The Godfather* did save my lunch money and shield me from bodily harm on more than one occasion as a kid. More than thirty-five years ago, I came under his generous protection and, although I've never properly repaid him, if he were alive today (or ever), he'd have the undying loyalty and gratitude of myself and dozens of other Italian American nerds from the Bronx, in circa 1972.

Godfather and Guardian Angel, Vito Corleone. In the Bronx in the 1970s, the specter of Vito Corleone shielded me from schoolyard muggings (Marlon Brando as Vito Corleone in *The Godfather*, Paramount Pictures, 1972).

Francis Ford Coppola's Godfather Saga influenced a generation of filmmakers with its amazing balance of visual beauty and realism. It introduced us to the next generation of great actors (Pacino, DeNiro, Duvall, Caan) and gave us the signature performance of Marlon Brando's brilliant career.

But it also saved me from handing over my lunch money every day to my thuggish schoolmates, thus ensuring that my wonder years were fueled with ample amounts of Beef-A-Roni and buttered rolls, instead of black eyes and bloody noses. And as an adult, Don Vito saved my job on multiple occasions and got me some nice raises and some phony baloney title bumps; and when my last job ultimately went away for good, he secured me a pretty good severance package and a nice parting letter. And all I did was take his advice.

I was saved as a kid because, thanks to the dazzlingly beautiful, yet realistic, world depicted in the movie, the myth of Mafia omnipotence seemed incontrovertible, which made Italians a little bit scarier to other groups. Before the release of *The Godfather*, many people even questioned whether a so-called "Mafia" existed. Francis Ford Coppola's brilliant adaptation of Mario Puzo's best-selling epic novel not only erased the "so-called" prefix from the term "Mafia" for all time, it also portrayed a Mafia that was more pervasive, powerful, and threatening than previously conceived.

The Mafia was not only real, they were scarier than we could have imagined. They were a menacing, manipulative subculture, with its fingers in all slices of the American Pie, from banking to show biz to politics. They were everywhere at once, sometimes a dark force, other times a beacon of protection—a combination of the CIA and the Super Friends.

Thanks to that uptick in overall Italian "street cred," I went from being a perpetual mid-day snack for the cafeteria predators to an "untouchable."

"Leave him alone, he's Italian," I heard one would-be mugger advise another, who had me in a headlock and was about to shake my fillings loose. "Leave him alone or the Mafia will kill you." It wasn't true, of course, but nobody wanted to take the chance.

All at once, in 1972, at age thirteen, I was someone to steer clear of. I was an Italian. Almost overnight, my premature moustache and my thick, sprawling eyebrows, un-mistakable genetic markers of my hundred-percent Italian heritage, were like warning signs to potential assailants—like the bright coloring of a poisonous tree frog.

"Hands off," the eyebrows said, "or something really *bad* will happen to you."

The highest-grossing movie of all time had my back, and I needed it. Most Italian kids in the Bronx were tough enough to throw down with any would-be assailant. Kids like Benny DiMarco and Johnny Benino would spar with anything from mailboxes to Oldsmobiles. Their parents would often encourage them to fight to keep them out of "real trouble" or as a way to take in some fresh air.

I, on the other hand, took the words "mama's boy" to new heights. Instead of a sandwich for school, my mother packed me a fresh umbilical every day. Chubby, baby-faced, sporting a Rubber Soul-era Beatles haircut and typically dressed in blue Pro-Keds and green pants, I might as well have worn a "Mug Me" sign taped on my back.

I needed the protection of an avenging angel and, in 1972, he appeared in the form of Vito Corleone. Quiet, cool, and lethal,

1. *Fredo vs. Frodo*

Vito Corleone put a bullet in the head of the stereotypical image of Italians. Before *The Godfather*, that image was comical, loud, and dim-witted, and could be summed up in two words: Chico Marx. But as hysterical as he was, the image of a vengeful Chico Marx did little to deter the neighborhood toughs from their near daily shakedown of me. Don Corleone was a different story. In the mind's eye of the American public, we Italians went from apple salesmen and garbage truck drivers to intelligent, ruthless power brokers with immeasurable wealth and influence.

That's quite a leap in coolness quotient. *The Godfather* not only made it cool to be Italian, but also to be a criminal. In my neighborhood, we would play *The Godfather* instead of cops and robbers, with the last kid picked being forced to play Fredo or, worse, movie mogul Woltz asleep in his bed.

To this day, millions of American men of all backgrounds are still playing *The Godfather*, quoting Parts I and II incessantly, and driving their spouses insane. When it comes to inspiring dialogue-quoting legions, Coppola's masterpieces rank with *Star Wars*, *Star Trek*, and the *Lord of the Rings* series. I personally know dozens of people who can dispense dialogue for any scene you can throw at them from both Part I and Part II.

> Frankie Pentangeli and Michael argue: *"Mi familia no mangia en Las Vegas y no mangia en Miami, con Hyman Roth."*
> Michael and Tom at the funeral: *"It's a smart move. Tessio was always the smart one."*
> Captain McCluskey as The Turk searches Michael for a gun: *"I've frisked a thousand young punks."*
> Vito at the funeral home: *"Well, my friend, are you ready to do me the service?"*

We are a close-knit group, this cult of Corleone, able to hold entire conversations in our native tongue: Corleonic. We amuse each other endlessly, and on the rare occasion when we surprise each other with an arcane bit of dialogue, we celebrate like archeologists who've uncovered a Pompeian sub-division.

We are a "family." And may that family live a hundred years. However, when I looked objectively at this "family," I noticed we all had two things in common:

1. We admired the Corleones for their guts, wealth, and power.
2. None of us *had* any guts, wealth, or power.

None of the compulsive Corleone quote-machines I knew could be considered major successes in anything we did. This led me to two more conclusions:

1. Genuinely successful people don't devote their lives to watching *The Godfather* and then quoting it over and over (this generally applies to *Lord of the Rings*, *Star Trek,* or *Star Wars* too).
2. None of us learned anything valuable from watching *The Godfather* movies over and over.

I came to realize that the most slavish *Godfather* fans were, for the most part, just as mediocre as the guys in Spock ears, Darth Vader helmets, or Gandalf the White robes. It was a sad revelation.

"Godfather nerds" were merely "nerds."

It made me ask, "Why?" Our heroes weren't spacemen or wizards. They were successful, albeit unorthodox businessmen who lived in the real world. You can see where a Darth Maul wannabe would struggle as a bond trader or a tax attorney. But why were *we* struggling? Our hero, Vito Corleone, was the king of kingpins. Yet, judging by their tax returns, the disciples of Don Vito had learned nothing about business from their hero.

So while the Corleones were outsmarting crooked U.S. senators, we, their devotees, were wrestling with paper jams. While Michael was strong-arming an old-time casino owner, we, his disciples, were fighting over the last jelly donut in the box. We would watch Sonny try to run a crime empire *and* win a gang war, yet our idea of multi-tasking was to put a box around a piece of clip-art while counting our sick days.

We were watching, but we weren't learning. Watch *The Two Towers* a hundred times and you will never get so much as a hint of how to fatten your paycheck. Yet, it's all there in *The Godfather*—how to fight and win, how to outguess your foe, how to be *successful*. This is the unique value-add of *The Godfather* movies, yet most of us haven't taken advantage. So it's time to do more than just thrill to *The Godfather* movies. It's time to stop *reciting* the dialogue and start *living* it.

The Corleones were smart and disciplined and always a step ahead of their competition. But what made them so successful? Why were they meta-Mafia?

The Corleones had a core game plan and used it to defeat their rivals over and over. That game plan can help us succeed or, at the very least, feel more secure in our workplaces if we can identify it and apply it.

Talk about "entertainment value." These movies can enrich our lives and our wallets. Watch Fredo and you'll learn how personal weakness can cost you a fortune. Watch Frodo and you'll learn what? How to run in giant rubber feet? Frodo may be the more likeable, but you'll learn more watching Fredo snivel than watching Frodo gazing dewy-eyed at Sam. In these trying economic times, whom would you rather have on your side: Tom Hagen, the Consigliere, or Gimli the Dwarf?

With this book, I've tried to distill the more universal lessons. These are lessons that can be applied to any business— while being perfectly legal. Being a Corleone is not only about the birthright. It's about the mindset. And assimilating their thought processes is the core of what we'll do here.

We will identify the core values that gave the Corleones their inner strength. We'll learn decision-making techniques, such as WWVD (What Would Vito Do?), and in the process, we'll make Vito Corleone our personal success coach. While some people swear by Dr. Phil, I'm going with Dr. Vito. Do you want to "get real" or "get real smart"? Seems like a no-brainer to me.

We'll learn a meeting methodology called H.A.G.E.N. that states that no meeting, no matter how critical, need ever last more than ten minutes. If the heads of the five families can settle a gang war in five minutes, why do you need two hours to decide whether to buy a new web server or not?

We'll learn that the existence of "friends" in the workplace is a myth and that people's behavior can be predicted with relative certainty, once you've properly classified the relationship. Don't worry about losing friends. You never had any in the first place.

We'll journey inward. By taking the Corleone test, you'll find out who you are and how that can help or hurt you. We will learn the secrets of controlling our emotions in the workplace. Wouldn't you like to have Vito's ability to read people? Or have Michael's emotional control and flair with a lit cigarette?

Other books will teach you negotiation, emotional control, or meeting facilitation. But while other business books are falling over themselves trying to create metaphors to help you visualize things, our visuals are from arguably the greatest movies of all time. There's no "Chicken Soup" needed for our soul. No parables about misplaced cheese. If you ever need an example of what we're talking about in a particular chapter, pop in the DVD, pull up a chair, and watch success in action.

We'll show you the world as Vito likely saw it. It's a darker, more cynical place than most self-help books portray, but it will sound more familiar to you. While other self-help books take the view that there is something in you that needs improving, we take the view that regardless of your abilities, everyone around you in business is a bastard and it's better to understand how they think than try and fix your own shortcomings.

It's a cold and calculating outlook, but that's the business world, a world where everyone is out for himself and no one is interested in a greater good. Let the other nerds go on quoting "the prime directive." The Force can be with them. The cash stays with us. For the price of this book, it's an offer you really can't refuse.

Sorry, we had to say it at least once.

On a personal note, Don Corleone, this book is my clumsy, Luca Brasi-ish way of thanking you for all you did for me and all the Italian kids of JHS 127 in the Bronx. The tough kids, the sissy kids, kids who climbed on rocks—all of them— owe you. For all the Oscar Mayer hot dogs, Beef-A-Roni, and fish sticks you saved me, and the beatings and torn collars you spared me, I thank you for your protection.

Sorry, Frodo, Spock, Obi-Wan, and Yoda. You guys weren't there when I needed you most...at work. I tried being virtuous, high-minded, and brave, but ended up frustrated, passed-over, and miserable. In life, I'll listen to my heart, or to The Force, but when it comes to business, I'm best served listening to my Godfather.

* * *

2. It's Not Personal— It's Strictly Business

TOUGH TIMES REQUIRE TOUGH PEOPLE. But these times? This is almost most unfair.

These are ugly economic times—bankruptcies, bubbles, bailouts, and Bernie Madoff; plunging stock prices and Ponzi schemes; double-digit unemployment; astronomical, un-pay-able deficits. Every economic headline is groaning under the weight of superlatives: "BIGGEST crisis since…" "MOST FORECLOSURES in California," "LARGEST one-month job loss…."

There's no end in sight and no safe haven. No place to make money and no completely safe place to keep it—not in housing, nor the stock market, not even in banks anymore. The American economy is tapped out and maxed out. Treasury Bond yields, an indicator of America's credit worthiness indicate that as a country, we couldn't even qualify for a Macy's charge card.

Tough times, but as our leaders tell us, Americans are tough, resilient people. "When the going gets tough, the tough get going," or so the saying goes. You pick yourself up by the boot-straps, put on a happy face, and get back in the fight.

But these days, it seems like the fight is rigged. Unfair. If you have a job, you're way ahead of a lot of people, but you need to fight like hell to keep it. Ten years ago, pre-Y2K, the best method to secure your job was to threaten to leave it. Nowadays, even doing your job well isn't enough to secure it. The rules in corporate America have changed, and in some cases broken down, along with the economy. Hard work, loyalty, and integrity just don't pay off like they used to.

You can work your way up in a corporation, only to find that your higher salary "exposes" you to a layoff. You can pour everything into your company, only to find that your bosses have been stealing from the company or letting it rot so they can be bought out. One day, you read that your company is reporting red ink; the next, that your CEO got a record bonus and is dating a Kardashian.

You think to yourself, *Crooks!* And you'd be right. They are crooks. They always have been. They've always been stealing from their employees, their stockholders, and their customers. These days, they're just less subtle—more audacious. Today, the swindlers make off with *billions* of dollars and affect millions of lives. And they keep evolving. We think we've got them regulated, but every year, newer and smarter scoundrels keep popping out of the ooze.

Meanwhile, closer to Earth, your managers, your "leaders," are too busy fighting for their own jobs to worry about your needs. Worse, in some cases, they are pushing you out the door to ease the headcount pressure on them. You can sense their blood lust as they size you up, looking at you as if work were a desert island cartoon scenario and you were a giant hot dog. One slip-up and they'll push a button on you. And your colleagues? Your brothers and sisters in the trenches? Once comrades-in-arms, they are now pointing their bayonets at you. Unfair.

You need to get tough, and not just plucky, "can-do" tough. Not stick-to-it tough, or "Move My Cheese" tough. None of those Up with People, keep on swimming, Norman Vincent

Peale platitudes seem to work anymore. That's because the rules in business have changed. You're dealing with crooks, thieves, liars, and sneaks. And those are the guys on *your* side. They are your co-workers, your supervisors, and your employees. You're having lunch with these people, for God's sake. You need to think like they do, or at least understand and anticipate where they are coming from, if you're going to keep them in your sights.

* * *

When it comes to criminal businessmen, Vito Corleone and his family are the American gold standard. The Godfather himself was as mentally tough a character as we've ever seen on screen. He needed to be. We're in a profound economic crisis, but imagine what Vito Corleone had to overcome. He grew up in a world with no TARP bailouts, no Social Security, no eBay to sell knick-knacks on, no Suze Ormon, and worst of all, no Jim Kramer.

Fighting with alley cats for scraps from a garbage can, running from bandits, perverts, and cutthroats, this was life on the Lower East Side around the turn of the twentieth century for an orphaned, immigrant nine-year-old.

Life must have been one big, long knife fight for young Vito. But not only did he survive, he rose to become king of the underworld. This was a tough guy. Tough and admirable, and a winner. Vito is the guy that Donald Trump imagines he is.

His fortune was immeasurable. His financial interests were diverse and flourishing. His influence was widespread. But Vito was also a genuine family man—a doting father and loyal husband. In a crazy, twisted way, Vito had the life we all

2. *It's Not Personal—It's Strictly Business*

wanted: a big, loving family; lots of wealth; really cool friends; relative peace of mind.

He sounds like a guy who had achieved what we call today "work-life balance."

Vito and his family did unspeakable things in the name of business—extortion, robbery, murder—and, apparently, they could leave it all at the office come 5 p.m. They knew how to separate business from personal, how to keep emotions out of it.

Their mantra was: "It's not personal. It's strictly business." That was the litmus test for their actions. If it's personal, it's bad. Don't do it. If it's "business," then, hey, it's good! Jump right in and get started. It's a simple rule and one that's easy to remember.

To the Corleones, or anyone else with a life or death occupation, like an astronaut, airline pilot or 7-11 owner, the ability to separate business from personal is key to sustained success. When you're landing your plane in the Hudson, or to trying to print thirty dollars' worth of PowerBall tickets for a drunken lady living out of a shopping cart, the ability to suppress emotions is essential. The Corleones, who played for all the marbles every single day, needed to stay cool to stay in business.

So if it worked in an organized crime environment, or on a disabled airliner, why wouldn't it work in accounting or something really dangerous like, outside sales?

It's not personal. It's strictly business. What we call "murder," Michael or Vito would call a "transaction." Consider the famous baptism day massacre in *The Godfather, Part I.* If Michael Corleone was stressed out that day, it was over having enough cold cuts for the folks back at the house after Mass.

The multiple murders part was just "working on a Sunday" for Michael.

There was no room for emotion in the Corleone's business. Whenever they recognized emotionality in one of their own (for example, Fredo), he was marked as weak or inconsequential or, worse, sent out to live in Las Vegas. In the 1950s, Las Vegas might as well have been Mars with free drinks and Johnny Mathis. Fredo Corleone was *sensitive* and, in that era, in that family, in that business, being sensitive meant you ended up either in the kitchen with the women or at the Desert Inn. But never in the mix as far as the business went.

Any show of emotion over a business matter was unthinkable. When a weepy Johnny Fontaine asks Vito for help, the Godfather practically slaps the olive oil voice out of his throat. Psychiatrists call it "compartmentalization": the ability to keep important aspects of your life or personality separate. When Vito exhorted Johnny to "act like a man!" what he was really saying was, "You should compartmentalize. That will help you tackle these business problems without the burden of emotionality!"

It's not personal. It's strictly business. Some would say this phrase represented their lack of humanity, their soullessness. Sure, there's some merit to that, but that doesn't mean we can't benefit from the notion of separating our emotions from our work. Some would call their ability to separate themselves from their deeds *"psychosis"* or *"mania."* You say *"tomato...."*

If soullessness works, I say be soulless.

Coming to Your Emotional Rescue

The biggest obstacle to success for most of us is the inability to control our emotions in the workplace. Many of us have the equivalent of a nervous breakdown at least once per day. We know we shouldn't, but every day we let the workplace and its stresses devour us.

Each morning, we drive up to the office, take a deep breath, and say, "Today I'm not going to blow up; today will be a good day." Then you get that queasy feeling in your stomach. That's not your Egg McMuffin heading for the exits. That's your soul telling you, "I don't want to be here; it hurts to be here."

You walk in, trying to keep an open mind and a happy face. But you know it won't last because there is an avalanche of negative stimuli waiting to crush those good vibes like a Mack truck backing over an overripe peach. Typically:

- Your boss publicly shoots down every one of your ideas in a meeting. Meanwhile, you know that, two days later, she'll roll them out as her own.
- Gossipy employees send instant messages to each other about your expanding waistline or Texas-shaped bald spot.
- Arrogant young MBAs order you around like you're a rickshaw driver.
- Rumors of a layoff send everyone in your group scrambling for a lifeboat. Suddenly your once happy department has become *Lord of the Flies* and everyone is in a life and death struggle to survive.

You feel disappointment, betrayal, rage, hopelessness…and that's all by 9:45 a.m. You tell yourself to shrug it off, but you can't. You're simultaneously banging your head against the wall, while looking over your shoulder and thinking about running into a corner and punching something. (And your boss said you couldn't multi-task.) You're emotionally contorted, feeling completely ill at ease, while putting on a happy face. Many of us spend our workday in this psychological Cuisinart, our emotions in constant flux, yet constrained by notions of acceptable corporate behavior to portray an air of calm and command. You're being dismissed, ignored, passed over, or snickered at nine to ten hours a day, and you're expected to smile through it. This runs counter to our biological programming. If you get punched in the face in the real world, you're programmed to yell, "Ouch!" At work, you get punched in the face, and you're expected to say, "Thanks, Bob. Lunch?"

Who wouldn't go nuts in that environment?

Well, actually, Vito Corleone wouldn't. And that's what made him cool and rich. But you and I? We are addled to the point of uselessness by our negative emotions. We are turning on an emotional spit every hour, especially these days, when nobody's job feels safe anymore.

We exist in an emotional state that is one part Lucy Ricardo (overenthusiastic, childishly euphoric), one part Barney Fife (suspicious, cowardly), and one part Ricardo Montalban in *The Wrath of Khan* (vengeful, spiteful).

Living like this, working like this every day, can drive a person insane. In corporate America, many of us spend hours at a time with our actions in direct conflict with our feelings.

This conflict will not only keep you from succeeding, it will also drive many of you clinically mad. To control the madness, you self-medicate, or worse, you watch *Big Brother*.

Am I exaggerating when I use terms like "madness" or "insanity"? Strike up a conversation one day with a ten-year corporate veteran, especially one whose career stalled around 2001, and you'll get a glimpse of the *Heart of Darkness* they have passed through. It's an experience not unlike talking to a Vietnam vet who survived Thet. They are disconnecting with the rest of the world. Their eyes dart suspiciously, legs bounce nervously under their desk. They avoid eye contact and loud noises make them jump.

Others seem strangely at peace, smiling benignly. These are the ones who are self-medicating, rifling through their pockets for Xanax or Valium. You can spot them easily as they often find themselves at a printer, wondering aloud why they are there. Both types, the twitchy/angry ones and the sedated/drooling ones, have been exposed to years of psychic mortar fire in the workplace. They are trauma victims, abuse victims.

So ask yourself, do you want to end up like Vito Corleone, successful and at peace, or like Viet Cong-leone—traumatized and twitchy? Are you paying too high of an emotional tax every day? Is it affecting your productivity, happiness, and longevity (corporate and otherwise)?

How much could you get done if you weren't pissed off, sad, or suspicious all day? Wouldn't it be great if no one at work could hurt you? What could you accomplish if you had the Godfather's easy going style, coupled with his leonine menace? Or if you had Michael's ruthlessness, and ascot-wearing cool.

Time to shake the emotions, Misty. Cut them loose and you'll start to have some impact in the workplace. Let Vito,

Michael, and Tom Hagen be your guides to a new tranquility. We'll show you how to get there, but first, it helps to understand *why* we've become a nation of Khans, Lucys and Barney Fifes.

Corporate America: We Are Family (I Got All My Prisoners with Me)

How did we get here? We didn't start out as emotional Chihuahuas. We were all once fresh-faced, eager, forward-looking, courageous, and enthusiastic. How did we end up twitchy, bitter, and exhausted? How can the workplace have such control over our emotional stability?

Part of it has to do with the myth of the corporate family. Fortune 500 companies typically purport to be great big, happy "families." And when they aren't hitting you over the head with it, they are at least slipping it into your Kool-Aid. Corporate marketing teams and HR groups bend over backward to find ways to slip the word "family" into every self-promoting piece of corporate literature: "The General Foods family of companies"; "We respect families and work-life balance."

It sounds crazy, but when it comes to turning independent adult men and women into domesticated alpaca, the phony family scam really works. The Corleones understood the power of this dynamic. Their operatives were members of the Corleone crime "family". The "family" charade was created to squeeze the maximum amount of loyalty out of an employee base that was, at best, ethically wobbly. Do you think Vito really wanted to see Luca Brasi at his daughter's wedding, let alone spend one-on-one time with him? But Vito knew that to keep the family illusion credible, sometimes you have to play the part of patriarch.

Your management knows the same thing. Every once in a while, they take you to a ballgame, or sit in a dunk tank at a fundraiser, buy you some nachos at Chili's, or take a picture with your wife and kid. They are just playing the part of patriarch or matriarch, keeping you cowed and confused with talk and trappings of "family." The more attachment you feel, the more you'll push yourself.

Western civilization, particularly American culture, is rooted in the strength and peace derived from family. Nuclear family, just like nuclear weapons—are what makes America strong. Popular culture often reflects the idea that family is the only place you will find peace. Countless computer-animated family flicks are based on that notion. Ragtag bands of animals, be they dinosaurs or ducklings, find themselves orphaned, alone, then adopted and, through shared adversity, they find love and realize they've become a flock, a herd, a *family.*

So, the people we work with? They are our lovable, ragtag flock. Hank, your supervisor, is the grouchy mammoth. You are maybe the zany sloth or the sullen saber tooth. The work and the burdens we share? That's our adversity, and despite our differences, and because the company says so, it's us against them, with them being "the competition" or "poor performance indicators". We are a family! A herd!

When we buy into the fact that our co-workers and bosses are family, we convince ourselves that they'd never do anything to hurt us. After all, that kid in the cube in front is like a son to you; the veteran office manager is like everyone's whacky aunt. So when they do things to hurt us, we are mystified, pissed off, or heartbroken.

You can say to yourself, "Hey, every family has its ups and downs," and go back to your herd, or you can snap out of it.

You're at *work*, not on *Party of Five*. Snapping yourself out of the family trance is your first step toward freedom.

"Night of the Living Dead" or "Daddy's Home"

So after we run this emotional gauntlet every day, tortured or betrayed by our corporate family, what happens to us when we go home at night? What happens when we confront our real families? We act like zombies.

That's the saddest consequence of this dynamic. After spilling our guts for nine hours for our work "family," there's nothing left to give to our real families. We numb ourselves with alcohol or pills. We diddle on the Internet, chatting up equally messed-up thirty-eight-year-old guys from Gainesville pretending to be eighteen-year-old girls from Manila. We play on-line games to escape ourselves, becoming dark warriors or elves or wizards—people or at least "things" in control.

Our kids? We'll spend a half hour playing HALO with them, but our hearts aren't there and they know it. We still aren't sure which one is Master Chief.

The wife? She's lonely and looking for anyone to talk to. Instead, she gets you, the husk of the man she married, gutted, empty, and brittle as a Peruvian mummy. After spending nine hours a day in a state approximating a nervous breakdown, we have nothing left for the ones we are doing it all for.

It's Not Personal—It's Strictly Business (See? We got back to it.)

You need to reverse the emotional dynamic immediately. Think about Vito and all he accomplished by separating the business from the personal. Here was a man who could host a wedding, plan a beating on a sexual assailant, clean up an immigration mess, and harass an old-time studio exec all in one afternoon. Vito somehow held it all together. You'll need to learn how. And don't you dare suggest that your job is more stressful than his. He had an underworld crime empire to run, horses to decapitate. You? You just have three analysts and some guy in India to manage.

There's an old maxim that if you hear something often enough, you will start to believe it. Corporations try to do it with the term "family." The same thing happens when you repeat something to yourself often enough. We need to push out the stupid, distracting messages and insert the pertinent, Vito-esque messages. So every day when you get to work and the emotional turmoil starts, when the Egg McMuffin sings its angry song from inside your small intestine, the thing that you should repeat is: "It's Not Personal. It's Strictly Business"

Every time something unpleasant happens at work, remind yourself: "It's not personal. It's strictly business." Any time something *pleasant* happens, remind yourself: "It's not personal. It's strictly business."

And if you find yourself with a few minutes to kill on your hands, remind yourself: "It's not personal. It's strictly business." Start repeating this to yourself and you'll start to handle the emotions. You need to control all your emotions. Overly positive emotions can be a big distraction in the workplace as well.

Vito Corleone never got too high or too low, even as young Vito Corleone, as conceived by the typically volcanic Bobby DeNiro. It's interesting to note that the three breakout stars from the *Godfather* saga, DeNiro, Pacino, and Duvall, were never as controlled or calm on screen as they were when they were playing Corleones. Every subsequent performance by the Big Three has found them on a slippery slope of hammyness. Nothing they've done, particularly Pacino, has resonated with us like the cool and calculating Michael.

Corleone cool—it worked for Pacino. It will work for you.

No event, no matter how life-changing, ever rattled Vito. Vito landed in America...nice, but let's get to work. I have a knapsack to unpack.

Vito spent three months in quarantine...fine. Nice to have some alone time after a long, cramped voyage.

Control your feelings. Make everything "strictly business." Keep *It's Not Personal, It's Strictly Business* in the front of your mind and, guaranteed, all the things that drove you up a wall will be gently put aside like a cat that's spent too much time on your lap.

- Charlie took credit for your idea? No biggie. You'll have more ideas. Everyone knows Charlie is an idiot.
- You found out your "pal" to whom you spilled your guts invited your boss to lunch without you? Great. Now you know who your enemies are.
- The boss pulled you aside to tell you he sees great things in your future? Nice to hear, but it's meaningless until there's money or a title discussed.

It works, because it's true. It works because it's the only sane approach. Once upon a time, Vito Corleone had to take out the local neighborhood chieftain, Don Fanucci, in *The Godfather, Part II*. This was his first documented kill. If he had to wrestle issues of right or wrong, or conscience, or the fate of his eternal soul, it's likely that Vito might have let Fanucci off the hook. But once he boiled the question down to "Business? Si o No?" it became an easy choice.

Once you start believing in "It's not personal…" you see things differently—like having infrared goggles on, or acquiring vampire night vision. Suddenly, you're seeing things in people and situations you've never seen. In seeing things differently, you'll act differently. You'll become a force. You're a crouching tiger—quiet, patient, and formidable.

I have goose bumps for you. Remember, we're talking about not only *not* showing emotions, but also not feeling them either. "Not showing" emotions is what most of you have been doing. Many of you are pretty good at it, smiling when you want to push your face through a pencil sharpener. But you're still feeling the emotions that are tearing you apart.

Keep a "Vito" Talisman Handy

There will be times when your resolve is tested, when it can't help but seem personal. At times like that, it's helpful to have a JPEG of Vito or Michael that you can refer to—a touchstone or talisman to keep in mind when the sledding gets tough. Or maybe you want to be a little more inconspicuous. After all, you don't want the competition to know what you're up to and maybe start using, "It's not personal…" for themselves.

Next time you feel like you're blinking back a tear, ask yourself, "Do I really want to get slapped by Vito?" When you feel like flying into a rage, picture Michael's cool smirk whenever he went face to face with a foe.

Everyone's got some kind of talisman. Whether it's a picture of the kids, a stress ball, an award, an inspirational quote, or posters of half-drowned kittens peeking out of toilets. Make sure you have something Vito-related to help you refocus. Some people have a Dilbert mug. You'll have Vito's "mug."

Hey…you could keep a copy of the book in your cube. I'm just saying….

Benefits of "It's Not Personal…"

If you can say, "It's not personal…" and believe it, after a few weeks, I promise you the following will happen:

- You won't be emotionally drained at the end of your day. Your wife and kids will love to sit out on the stoop with the *new* you, like Vito and his young family did in their tenement home.
- Annoying workmates will cease to matter.
- Your focus will improve; thus, your productivity will, too. Did Vito ever miss a trick? Probably not. Even after he became semi-retired (after being semi-killed in *The Godfather, Part I*), the old Don was as sharp as a tack and three moves ahead of the competition.
- You'll sleep better. No more dreading certain people or situations because they anger you or terrify you.

The biggest one, "your focus and productivity will improve," can translate into money rather quickly in terms of bonus, promotion, or merit increase. When you filter out emotion and useless energy drains, you'll improve your productivity while actually decreasing the effort you put into your job. In other words, earn more while working less.

There. The book just paid for itself. Why not buy another for your buddy? This is just the beginning, but this is enough to make your work experience better for you and your family. In effect, you've given yourself a raise because the work got easier.

So, again, buy another book.

The Downsides of the "It's Not Personal..." Line

- **You will lose some false friends.** This actually isn't much of a downside. People who knew how to push your buttons and pretended to be friends won't be able to push them anymore.
- **You'll scare the crap out of some people.** Some people will see that you're no longer a sucker and are now a threat.
- **You might miss the adrenaline.** Some people get off on living on the edge, on feeling like they are falling off a cliff. It's a false high. People who like living on an edge will inevitably go off it. Lemmings go off cliffs. *People* film them going off cliffs. Be a *person—not a lemming.*

You don't need to become devoid of humanity like Mr. Spock or, say, Glenn Beck. You can have some fun. You can have compassion. You can even have a harmless flirtation or two. You can joke around. You can still go to happy hour, occasionally. Just make sure that you control the emotions instead of them controlling you. Save your emotions for your family and your home. The kids don't need a zombie. They need a dad. Your wife doesn't need an Andean sarcophagus for a husband (at least not another one).

Always remember and live, *It's Not Personal—It's Strictly Business.* Control your emotions and you'll be walking down a spiritual path alongside Vito, Michael, and, Tom Hagen. You'll feel "closeness" to them that you've never felt before. A feeling of rapture.

Oops. I've got to stop myself. Getting a little emotional.

* * *

3. I Got Your Secret...
Right Here!

A FEW YEARS AGO, A VIDEO CALLED *THE SECRET* BECAME A WORLDWIDE SENSATION, SELLING THIRTY-FIVE MILLION COPIES WHILE CREATING TWICE THAT NUMBER OF FALSE HOPES AND DELUSIONS. If you're not familiar with it, the gist of *The Secret* is that the universe is this living force that monitors your wishes and dreams and then ultimately grants them, provided you truly believe that the universe will grant them.

This makes the universe, according to *The Secret*, a very large, very old, constantly expanding version of Jiminy Cricket. When you wish upon a star, you will get anything you want. Sounds simple, but there's a catch. The catch is that you have to wish really, really hard. The universe, it seems, is governed by something called the "Law of Attraction," meaning that your thoughts or wishes will cause the universe to open up for you and you will "attract" fame, health, or wealth. But the universe doesn't want or appreciate a half-hearted wish. You have to pour your soul into it, otherwise don't waste the universe's time.

In other words, the writers of *The Secret* left themselves a loophole. If you ask the universe for that nice little flower shop, and don't get it, it must be your fault. You didn't wish hard enough.

Ridiculous? Sure. Profitable? Oh, yeah. Apparently, people really need to believe in a "secret," so they will even latch on to a preposterous one. However, there really is a secret, but it's not the marshmallow Fluff-a-nutter espoused in the video. The Corleones were wise to it and part of *their* secret was knowing that people were always looking for the "secret." The real lesson of *The Secret* is that people are desperate for a cosmic elevator to success.

But can thirty-five million people (not to mention the numerous Astro-visualization experts, harmonic astrologers and dream interpreters who appeared on *The Secret*) really be that wrong? Is there something to this "secret" stuff?

Is *The Secret* Real?

The simple answer is "No."

The correct answer is also "No."

But the people behind *The Secret* do a great job convincing you that there is something to it, employing the same kind of *DaVinci Code*-esque, phony, historical imagery and specious logic used so successfully on the History Channel where shows like "MonsterQuest" continue to flourish.

Go to www.thesecret.tv, watch the trailer, and you'll be hit with images of Beethoven, DaVinci, Lincoln, Emerson, Edison, and Einstein. The narrator intones, "Throughout history, all the great leaders, all the great thinkers, all the great achievers, had something in common." The trailer suggests that a secret society, the custodians of the "Law of Attraction," buried the wealth creation secret away from the common man's reach.

One part of this is certainly true. All the great achievers and thinkers did have something in common. **They were smarter and worked harder than the rest of us.**

The trailer insinuates that people like Abraham Lincoln, a man who taught himself to write with a stick and a pile of coal dust, believed that merely wishing would make all good things happen. So what happened during the Civil War? Did the "secret" slip his mind? Wouldn't that have been a good time to wish really hard for things—like peace? And wouldn't Beethoven, after losing his hearing, have pulled out his old "secret" scrolls to "attract" his hearing back?

To suggest that Lincoln, Beethoven, and others, used the "secret" to become Lincoln, Beethoven, and others, not only insults their intelligence, but yours as well. But the producers and publishers of *The Secret* banked on the fact many of us don't use, and some of us don't have, any intelligence. And it paid off nicely for them.

Noted "Secret-tologist" Abraham Lincoln. If Lincoln were really "Honest Abe," he would have told the rest of us about "The Secret" (Abraham Lincoln, Library of Congress National Archives).

The Law of "Extraction"

Back around 2005, during the height of Secret-mania, my wife and I were given a copy of *The Secret*. It was a tough time in our lives. We were struggling with finances. I was struggling with my health and hating my job. We certainly could have used a "secret." We were ready for some wealth, peace of mind, and wish fulfillment. We were ready for our "Secret-ions."

Anxiously, we popped in the DVD, held hands, lit candles, and prepared to embark on our cosmic voyage to success. After three and a half minutes, we were laughing, and *The Secret* was tossed behind our couch (where it remains to this day—hidden from the outside world).

The real genius behind the video and *The Secret* book lay in the producers' understanding of human nature. They knew that many people want an easy path to success, yet have no idea where that path starts. What's more, they know that many people are suspicious of those who are more successful than they are. "They must know something we don't"; "they must have a friend in the business"; "they are just luckier." This is known as the **Law of Crap**, but it's a subject for another book.

We have become a nation of complainers, finger pointers, and recidivists. We stand on the sidelines or make the same bad decisions over and over again, and we watch other people make money, then spend all our energy knocking them down instead of trying to own up to the simple truth that their success spells out.

The simple fact is that some people know how to create wealth. Some know how to become famous. Some are gifted with talent or brains or looks. And what's more, they aren't afraid to work hard in pursuit of their goals.

That's how people become successful, but let's face it: That's not that sexy of a "secret," especially when compared to the kindly Santa Claus-like Universe that *The Secret* espouses, one that will give us ten-speed bikes, PlayStations, and heal our psoriasis if we just kiss its ass enough.

Instead of working harder on what we do, we cast about looking for plausible quick fixes like *The Secret*. The producers of that video know enough about the rest of us to know that we just won't accept that Katie Couric or John Madden or The Jonas Brothers are smarter or work harder than us. The Corleones also understood that same thing about people and took it one step further.

The Corleones had a "secret" and it was called "**The Law of Extraction.**" Simply stated: **The universe will give you what you wish for—wealth, fame, power—if you are willing to fight for it, to pry it from the universe's clutches, to extract it, per se.**

To put it another way, the universe isn't going to hand you anything no matter how many karma vouchers you hold. But with so many people sitting around wishing for stuff, you can take all the stuff they want but aren't willing to fight for.

The Law of Extraction—the Corleone Saga is the story of people working hard, taking what they could, and fighting for more when they had to. Vito Corleone's story, his saga, has much more in common with Katie Couric's than with the self-sedating, feel-good, wishful thinking of *The Secret*.

Katie Couric, despite her airhead reputation, has more than a little "Vito" in her. This is a woman who broadcast her own colonoscopy, a procedure that has been known to make grown men cry for an epidural halfway through it. This is a woman who survived *Today Show* gossip storms, the loss of a husband,

and negotiated her way into the anchor spot on the *CBS Evening News*. When her ratings started to founder, Katie recognized a big, fat, low-hanging fruit in the form of Sarah Palin (a woman with Vito's aspirations but none of his work ethic and tenacity). She GRABBED that opportunity by the neck and sucker-punched the smirk right off of then rising star Palin. In a series of interviews broadcast over a few nights, Couric exposed the VP nominee to be ill informed, inarticulate, and testy. Katie not only saved her career, she put Sarah Palin on her heels for the rest of the election. Vito would have been proud of Katie.

Katie. Vito. Lincoln. They're all fighters and workers. Not wishers and dreamers. To be fair, *The Secret* did get one thing right, but almost by accident. If you really, really want something, you might get it, but only because you're going to work hard for it and not because the universe is going to throw you a "wish" bone. *The Secret* neglects to mention how hard you have to fight to make it big.

Young Vito and the Law of Extraction

The nine year old Vito (played with lazy-eyed perfection by Oreste Baldini) was the personification of the Law of Extraction. Here was a kid who, after seeing his family murdered, hid in a donkey cart to get to the docks of Sicily, then crossed the Atlantic at the age of nine.

Most nine-year-olds today can't even cross over the couch to get a juice box without asking their parents for help. But Young Vito, speaking no English and with likely very little cash, established a beachhead in New York City. Ten years later, his franchise was up and running. This was after being called "dim-witted" by his mother in front of a bunch of strangers. Ouch.

We weren't witnesses to his maturity, but we must assume that Vito was the ultimate opportunist, because by the time he had grown into young Robert DeNiro, he had a job, friends, a wife and child, and on occasion could spring for a nice pear for the Missus.

Vito learned quickly. He observed the presiding neighborhood Mafia[1] kingpin, the oafish, overbearing Don Fanucci (the hilarious and spooky Gaston Moschin). Whereas others cowered at Fanucci's bluster, he saw Fanucci's bullying as a sign of weakness. When he and Fanucci finally butt heads, Vito retracted his claws and took what was his.

His comrades clearly didn't have the guts to take the next step, or they would have, years ago. Clemenza (Bruno Kirby, of *When Harry Met Sally*) was content to stuff his face with spaghetti and pay Fanucci full price. Young Tessio (John Apera), a nice-looking fellow, was content to pay Fanucci and sit around and wait inertly. Inevitably, he morphed into Abe Vigoda.

Only Vito took the chance. The other two didn't even have the courage to ask what Vito's plan was. Vito swooped down, taking what the other two didn't even see lying at their feet, which was opportunity (and, later, Fanucci).

Minestrone Soup for the Soul: Below is the first in our series of "Minestrone Soup for the Soul" stories. These are inspiring, true stories of people in the workplace who have overcome challenges using the business and behavior principals practiced by the Corleones. The first "serving" deals with the Law of Extraction and is called "The Bottleneck Opener."

---

1   Instead of the term "Mafia," I prefer the much more inclusive "Criminal American."

Many people in accounting hated Tranh. He was a bastard through and through. But he was the only one who knew how to update the system every month, so everyone was dependent on him. This made him not only a bottleneck, but also an overworked one, which made him even more of a bastard. Steve saw an opportunity here. He offered to help Tranh every month to share the load and improve efficiency. This would also increase Steve's value to the department.

Tranh would have none of it. Every month, he made sure that he started the process without Steve, so that Steve would have to wait another month to schedule time with him. When that month rolled around again, Tranh would of course agree to show Steve the system then once again kick it off on a Sunday evening, or when Steve wasn't remotely around.

Steve knew he was getting the run around. He, like a lot of people, had his fill of Tranh. Even management was sick of him; unfortunately, management wouldn't support Steve in his attempts to loosen Tranh's stranglehold. They hated Tranh, but were dependent on him and were afraid of antagonizing him. Tranh had a reputation for spitefulness and when things didn't go his way, or he felt pressure or interference, suddenly there would be problems and delays in the reporting process.

Steve couldn't make any headway, yet here was this great opportunity. He remembered the Law of Extraction and decided to fight for what he thought was right, as he knew Vito or Katie Couric would. He placed an anonymous call to the internal audit and compliance group, explaining the risks of all the financial reports going through a single, unreliable resource, namely Tranh.

A week later, internal auditors appeared requesting meetings with Tranh. In subsequent weeks, auditors ordered Tranh to document his procedures and to cross-train a second resource for backup and efficiency.

Naturally, Steve was selected, so Tranh was forced to train him. Steve did an excellent job with the process and, what's more, he was easier to work with than Tranh. Management decided to move more responsibilities over to Steve, who was given an eighteen percent raise later that year and an excellent review. Tranh quit the following year.

By fighting for what he knew was right, and what was good for him, Steve helped himself and his organization...and screwed Tranh.

Michael Corleone and the Law of Extraction

The Law of Extraction doesn't just apply to moments when you recognize opportunity. It applies during times when you have to defend what's yours. When Michael was called before the Senate committee and nearly charged with perjury, what did he do?

Did he sit in his recliner, take a deep, cleansing breath, and ask the universe for assistance with his problems? No. He got Frankie Pentangeli's brother on a plane from Sicily and whisked him over to the states for Frankie, the FBI, Congress, and the Associated Press to see.

Michael's statement to the committee had the right note of Law of Extraction defiance: "I challenge this committee to produce any witness or any evidence against me." It wasn't, "I really, strongly hope and envision that this committee, in co-operation with the universe, will open itself up to me and clear me of these false charges."

When you're in trouble, the universe is not going to come to your rescue, no matter how many karma vouchers you may hold. You have to fight. Don't be a victim. Roll up those sleeves and get ready to throw down.

We went through a lot in this chapter. It was necessary to check your commitment to reality-based self-help. Before we go any further, let's review:

1. Who gained great fortune via the Law of Attraction?
   a. Lincoln
   b. Churchill
   c. Henry Ford
   d. The producers / authors of *The Secret*

2. Your boss tells you he is going to transfer and that they are likely bringing in Ajay from Phoenix to replace him. You think that job should be yours. You should:
   a. Tell him you're the guy for the job and here are five reasons why.
   b. Go home, reach out to the universe with your soul, and attract that job.
   c. Tell your boss that if Ajay gets promoted, you'll support him. When Ajay gets here, show him what a great team player you can be.

Answers 1: d, 2: a

Summary:
- There is no Law of Attraction. The universe won't give you anything.
- The Law of Extraction states that the universe will give you things if you fight for it.
- Katie Couric and Vito Corleone had more in common than Abe Lincoln and the keepers of "The Secret."

* * *

4. Corleone School of Communications

As directed by Francis Ford Coppola and personified by Marlon Brando, Vito Corleone is a galvanizing figure. When he's on screen, we can't take our eyes off him. When he's off screen, we're drumming our fingers waiting for his return. We cherish every moment we have with him. This is a character that SPEAKS to us. And when Vito finally keels over in the tomato patch, a victim of a hyperactive grandkid with a loaded DDT can, we miss him terribly.

Vito Corleone: Superstar

More than thirty-five years after he stepped out of the pages of Mario Puzo's novel, we are still mesmerized by the sight of Vito, as brought to life by Marlon Brando. Amazingly, this serendipitous piece of casting almost never happened.

Reportedly the Paramount brass was upset with the idea of casting the tempestuous and semi-retired Brando in the highest-profile movie role since Scarlet O'Hara. Paramount executives were leaning toward Ernest Borgnine or Orson Wells.

We'll never know if we dodged a cinematic bullet when Paramount relented to let Brando test for the role. Ernest Borgnine may have been up to it. Orson Wells, to be fair, had spent the last ten years playing behind-the-scenes heavies in

A Touch of Evil and *A Man for all Seasons*. For the life of me, I can't see him chasing his grandson with an orange peel in his mouth, but what do I know? Apparently, Francis Ford-Coppola knew enough to go to the mat hard for Brando, and the rest is cinematic history.

Why Do We Love Vito?

The Godfather was a man who lived above the law. But what makes this inherently evil man fascinating and even like-able to us, as opposed to other dark, power-mad forces like, say, **Dick Cheney**?

What makes some dark, manipulative characters scary and others lovable? Darth Vader, much like Don Vito, was love-able. Dick Cheney on the other hand, will never end up on a kid's lunchbox.

When Dick Cheney speaks, he clicks down the thermostats on millions of souls around the world. He's a dark force like Vito, but lacking that certain "something." Conversely, when a **Darth Vader** stares out from behind those black, plastic, yet somehow sad eyes, we are hooked. Vader was a half-mechanical brute with dark powers and dreams of conquest, and yet he ended up on kids' sneakers and underwear.

But while Vader hooks us with those soulful, lonely, fiberglass eyes, **Vito hooks us with his communication skills.** Quiet communication skills are Vito's dark magic. It's one thing to conquer the world; it's another to do it while conquering the world's heart as well. Don Corleone is a man with a PhD in body language. A man of a few well-chosen words, a man of pith. His communication skills are as effective as any Jedi Mind Trick, but better, because we can actually reproduce them.

In terms of movie history, Vito Corleone's ability to say more with less ranks him up there with Charlie Chaplin's *The Little Tramp.* But while emulating Vito's communication style will get you places in the business world, acting like The Little Tramp will get you a medical leave.

It's always important to pick the *right* movie mentor to emulate.

Conversational "Space": Your First Frontier

We live in a three-dimensional universe (this shouldn't be news to any of us). Objects have length, width, and depth. Some physicists talk about the three dimensions existing in a fourth "location dimension": a dimension of space.

Conversations have the same three dimensions:
- Length: how long you are talking about something
- Width: how many subjects you will cover
- Depth: how deep you will go into one subject

Clever, huh? These are the three dimensions of conversation. There is also a fourth dimension of conversation: the "space" of a conversation. In this space, you'll find the pauses, the body language, the looks, the raised eyebrows—all the non-verbal communication.

Vito **"owns"** the space in every conversation he's in. Vito's power derives from his calm. He is never agitated. He seems focused and formidable. He keeps his body quiet—no distractions, no indications. No "tells." We live in a post-World Poker Tour environment, now, where everyone who's ever played a hand of Hold 'Em thinks he can read his opponent. Watch Vito in his big meetings in *Godfather I*. Is there any indication of what he's thinking before he says it?

With his command of his body, Vito mesmerizes his opponents, like a boa constrictor staring down a tapir. He can turn a conversation on a gesture, a look, or a pause. Some examples:

- **He stands:** At the meeting with the heads of the five families, Vito **stands** up when he gives his warning to any and all to keep their hands off of Michael and to pledge commitment to the peace process. That small gesture, the act of standing, said to the other attendess, that his words were more than a threat. It would be backed up by force. In effect, it became "The Vito Doctrine."
- **He smiles:** In *The Godfather, Part II*, when young Vito is ambushed in his truck by Don Fanucci, who tells Vito he wants to "wet his beak," Vito smiles. That little show of civility must have sent a chill down Fanucci's spine. Fanucci sensed that Vito

wasn't intimated now, nor would he ever be. Or he may have thought, *Dimwit.*

- **He wipes:** During his meeting with The Turk, before he turns down his proposal, he sits next to him and brushes a few crumbs from his chair. A gentle sign of respect, a little soft personal contact from a fatherly figure who is about to break bad news to a younger man.

Gentle, quiet, and effective. Vito's ability to portray gentility and strength comes from his understanding of the work-life balance (chapter 1) or, as we know it, *It's Not Personal—It's Strictly Business.* He gets his support and strength from his family. With a balanced foundation at home, Vito can relax at work, and converse with a clear conscience and calm physical presence.

In chapter 1, you learned to stop reacting to your "work family" and start living with your real family. If you're walking that walk, that paradigm shift should have already produced some results in terms of feeling calmer at work.

With the genuine calm, you can work on quieting down your body and polishing up your presence to improve your control of conversation space. Some tips to ratchet up your inner Vito quotient:

1. Rehearse in a mirror—don't laugh. And don't stuff your face with cotton balls and do Brando. But as you rehearse anything, so shall you perform. Imagine yourself in conversation with your craziest boss; say, the creepy guy who keeps staring under the table at your feet, or the crazy lady who uses the actual French accented pronunciation for words

like "croissant" or with your nastiest, whiniest employees. Are you twitchy, edgy, or overly chatty? Then rehearse those tendencies out of you. Get into character and stay there.

2. Upgrade the wardrobe. Get yourself down to the Men's Wearhouse or to the Big and XXL Tall Shop and buy some nice suits, nice shoes. What are nice shoes? Easy. Find a pair of shoes that you like and if the price makes you say, "Holy crap. I'm not paying THAT for shoes!" then those are the shoes you need to buy. Successful people have known this "shoe formula" for generations. Can you picture Sonny or Michael in Payless? Even when Vito wasn't making it, he put an effort into dressing his very best.

3. Practice LISTENING with stillness. The Sioux warriors called this skill "Wat-tan-she," or "quiet breeze." Okay, no they didn't—but, even so, the ability to listen without talking over someone or looking like you are about to have a nervous breakdown is a skill that many of us don't have. Practice it on your kids. If you can sit for a half hour while your kid is running down what he wants for his birthday AND why he wants it without fidgeting, then you can handle anything.

Vito Space vs. Hyper Space (Sonny)

Vito's kids occasionally needed to take some lessons from the master. Sonny Corleone (James Caan) was the hothead of the Corleone family. His communication style was pure confrontation. And although he seemed to get a kick out of his volatile image, Sonny's lack of implacability also made him tactically vulnerable, a position Vito would never put himself in.

When Sollozzo the Turk kidnapped Tom Hagen, Sollozzo noted, "Sonny was hot for my deal." Sonny was incapable of playing close to the vest and anxious to share his opinion—the Mafia's version of an "American Idol" judge.

As a conversationalist, Sonny tries to control his territory with belligerence and his success rate is spotty at best. Shortly after the famous opening between Vito and Bonosera, we see Sonny and his wife, Deana (Marlana Hall), at the wedding reception. Their body language screams mutual suspicion and resentment.

> Sonny: Hey, Deana. Do me a favor. Watch the kids. Don't let 'em run wild, all right?
> Deana: Well, you watch yourself, all right?

Meaning, "Sonny, keep your ziti in the tray for once." Sonny slinks off, exasperated. His expression is pursed into what is commonly known as a "puss," which tells us that he loses most of these arguments with the missus.

What we learn right away is that not only is Sonny a poor communicator, he's not much of a family man, either. The relationship between family stability and business acumen is once again demonstrated here.

Overall, Sonny probably loses more than his share of conversations. Tom Hagen (Robert Duvall) gave him a few verbal spankings in *The Godfather, Part I* and to a genius like Michael (Al Pacino), Sonny's mind was easier to change than a light bulb. Volatile, emotional communicators have poorly formulated logic behind their arguments. Their supporting arguments are usually based on the following premise:

"But…but…you're ugly!"

They may be right, but typically this kind of argument can't stand up to cross-examination. So they often concede defeat in conversation. Volatile people make enemies. Enemies kill you. Sonny's demise was a foregone conclusion – a mathematical certainty.

So ask yourself, "In a tough conversation, am I more Vito or Sonny?" A lot of us have a little Sonny in us; we take pride in tweaking people. Or we hit the ejector button on unpleasant conversations because we're feeling hurt, angry, or dismissive.

Learn to identify moments when your Sonny tendencies are bubbling to the surface, then step outside and stuff some toilet paper in your cheeks and do Brando for a minute or two. Recognize when your argument isn't an argument at all, but pure emotion, like Sonny's. Later in the book, we'll talk about managing strong emotions in "Your Sonny Disposition."

Learning to quiet your mind and body like Vito can give you more control of a situation, a better chance at winning conversations, and surviving toll booths on the Long Island Expressway.

Space Saver No. 1—Maintaining a Pithy Mood

Vito, Michael, and Tom were masters of **pith**. "**Pithiness**" means an ability to get to the "core" or "central point" of a matter concisely. Pithiness was what elevated Vito and even Michael to criminal royalty. It's why we're quoting young Vito after all these years and not Jimmy from *GoodFellas* or Ace from *Casino*. Robert DeNiro played all three characters. He *underplayed* only one. Underplaying and leaving nonsense out of the conversation is the key to being effective.

How many of us begin sentences with, "It's like...like..." instead of just describing a situation? People use "I'm like..." instead of saying "I said...," as in "I was like 'are you kidding?'" to describe their responses in past tense. How many end every sentence with "you know"? These verbal tics are "white noise," conversational static. And like real static, they affect the reception of the message being transmitted.

Indifference for language is accelerating and creeping up to the highest levels of government. President George H. W. Bush was known for his convoluted, policy-wonk speak, but his son's tortured speech patterns have made the old man look like Gielgud at the Old Vic. Bush the younger likes to point out that his "Bushisms" in no way affected his ability to lead. Maybe he misspoke here, too. History's greatest leaders have been excellent speakers and writers. There are no calendars with funny "Lincolnisms." There are no T-shirts featuring the goofy "Churchillogic" or "Gandhi-gaffes."

President Obama has re-introduced the idea that the *president* of the United States should sound smarter than the regular *people* of the United States. He's not quite a Lincoln, but he may be Kennedy or even F.D.R. in his understanding that intelligent, well-reasoned oratory is a powerful political weapon. This was not a club that the Bushes liked to carry in their bag.

Great leaders *should* sound smarter than the guy in the Home Depot plumbing aisle. Leaders in general should.

Look to the most successful Corleones—Vito, Michael, Tom Hagen. Notice how none of them insert *any* static into their sentences. Neither did their most successful foes. Hyman Roth (Lee Strasburg), despite his diminished health, was as clear as a Sunday church bell. This could be the effect of great writing on the part of Mario Puzo and Francis Ford Coppolla. Look at the mugs in *Goodfellas*. Brilliantly written characters, but operating on a level or two beneath the Corleones in terms of verbal aptitude. The result? They are middle of the pack hoods, while the Corleones are the Rockefellers.

Does Hyman's fiery speech about the hit on his friend Mo Green have the same sizzle if it's spoken the way, well, you know, like, we speak?

"There was this, like, kid, ya know? He and I, like, totally grew up together. I, like, loved him. He and I, you know, made a fortune running molasses during the thing...the prohibition thing, you know? Like, your father did, too.

"He had this idea to, like, build a city at this, like, thing, this desert thing where the G.I.s go. He was a great man. A man with, like, total vision. And then I heard that someone put a bullet in his eye, ya know?

"I'm like, 'What?' Then I'm, like, 'OK. That's Mo. Talking headstrong, ya know?'"

This version of Hyman would have been feeding pigeons in the park in his golden years instead of nearly taking down Fidel Castro.

By sputtering out white noise, you lose the attention of your listener and control of your space. Being aware of the static you inadvertently insert into a conversation will help you control your space by making your points clearer to your adversary.

Space Saver No. 2—Defend Your Physical Space like It's a Territory

The conquest or control over a physical space is one of the fundamental measures of success. Even psychological control of that space is important. The Corleones divided their kingdom up into territories. The more territories they had, the better they were doing. Territories were what they fought for.

In the workplace, we wage little psychological battles every day. You compete with a co-worker for the one promotion slot. You battle in a meeting with a client who wants to blame your group for a project going south. You negotiate your merit raise with your boss.

Many of us fight these battles in a cubicle, but, oddly enough, it's a place we don't feel is worth fighting for. Sure, we have pictures of our kids. We have a poster of a drenched kitty in the toilet, but we see the cube as a symbol of our repression or ignominy. How can we impress or intimidate our adversary when we are sitting in a box, just another battery in the Matrix?

You have to learn how. Your workspace, no matter how small, is your battleground. Some of history's greatest battles have taken place over the smallest pieces of real estate—the Alamo, the OK Corral, Iwo Jima, Jon and Kate Gosselin's house.

In Corleonic terms, your cube is a territory. You work it. It pays off. You control it. And if anyone tries to muscle it from you, they should be in for a fight.

So next time your boss storms over to your cubicle breathing fire, or your nosy co-worker comes for a casual "visit" and starts fingering your in-basket, imagine yourself as Michael Corleone. How would Michael react to such an affront? Sometimes all it takes is a little visualization to get your mind right.

They are on your territory. Time to light the imaginary Michael cigarette, tie your imaginary ascot, and defend it like Michael would. Here are some psychological warfare tactics that will let either one of them know that you won't be bullied in your own little Alamo.

1. **Be on a phone call,** or pretend. Call yourself from your cell phone if you have to. Let them wait. Pretend to have a really good time on the call. After you hang up, don't apologize. Just shake your head and say something tantalizing like, "unbelievable."

2. **Offer the visitor a chair.** In fact, insist on it. If they insist on standing then you should immediately stand, too. You're re-enforcing the fact that you're civil and they aren't. That puts you on a higher moral plane. If you can't be in a higher salary grade, then a higher moral plane is almost as good. From a body language point of view, you don't want them looking down at you. Some of the crazier female bosses feel they need psychophysical advantages over their male employees, like standing over them or looking over their shoulders.

3. **Ignore their opening question and replace it with "How are you?"** If the boss opens with, "Is that analysis done yet?" you counter with, "How are you?" Two things can happen. He either calms down, which shows other people the influence you have on him, or he ignores your question and stubbornly repeats his. If aliens were watching you at that precise moment, they would assume that you, with your statesman's demeanor, are the manager.

Space Saver No. 3—Avoid "Active Listening"

From the **Study Guides and Strategies website (http://www.studygs.net)**, "Active listening intentionally focuses on who you are listening to...in order to understand what he or she is saying. As the listener, you should then be able to repeat back in your own words what they have said to their satisfaction."

Active listening also means inserting responses or prompts into a conversation to demonstrate to the speaker that you were "engaged." In a nutshell, active listening means repeating what a person just said to you, and saying things like "hmmm."

Other trigger phrases in the active listening tool kit include:

- Mm, hmm
- Oh, really?
- You're kidding!
- I see...
- (And, more recently) Awesome

This technique is known in the world at large as "**insincerity**" or "**phoniness**." Despite the good intentions of the motivational gurus who coined the phrase, active listening gives most people the distinct impression that they are *not* being heard. After all, all you are doing is waiting for a lull in the conversation to insert a limited set of responses, like a giant Magic 8-ball.

> **Speaker**: We've got some problems with the new policy file.
> **Active Listener / Magic 8-Ball**: Oh, really?
> **Speaker:** This is unacceptable. I'm going to send an email to Don.
> **Active Listener / Magic 8-Ball**: It is decidedly so...

We all know that Vito was no Magic 8-ball, nor was Michael, Tom, Hyman Roth, Senator Pat Geary, or Lou Woltz.

Watch Senator Geary and Michael lock horns and you get an idea of how formidable leaders should engage. When Michael takes a perfunctory stab at small talk and lobs a warm-up pitch to Geary ("Turnbull is a good man"), it's quickly swatted over the fence like a hanging curveball. Michael knows he's in a conversational knife-fight. And that's the way he likes it. Michael, knowing his foe is no push-over, dispenses with the niceties and responds with the now-famous counteroffer of, "Nothing. Not even the twenty thousand for the gaming license."

Active listening was not part of the Corleone playbook. People like to say listening is a skill. In fact, it is, but the skill involved in listening is "shutting up" and "paying attention." If you have an active listening page in your playbook, it's time to tear it out and burn it for good.

Vito and Bonosera: Active Listening in Action

To further illustrate how silly active listening sounds, we have a treat. **"The Active Listening Players"** will re-enact the famous first scene where Bonasera asks Vito to kill his daughter's assailants, this time with Vito portrayed as an active listening disciple. Let's listen in:

> **Bonosera**: I believe in America. America has made my fortune...
> **Active Listening Vito**: Mm, hmm. You're not from around here originally, are you?
> **Bonosera**: Um...no. Napoli. Anyway, I raised my daughter as an American...

Active Listening Vito: (nods appreciatively) Ahh, I see. As an American. A good old American girl. Awesome. Go on.

Bonosera: Don Vito, I gave her freedom, but I taught her never to dishonor her family.

Active Listening Vito: (nodding) Oh, really? So you just have the one girl, right? Linda?

Bonosera: One daughter. My poor Maria. But these animals...

Active Listening Vito: You're kidding! My one daughter, Connie, is getting married today. They grow up so fast.

Bonosera: Please, Don Corleone. These boys, they tried to take away her honor.

AL Vito: Mmmm, hmmm. And you want justice. Do you want some ziti?

Bonosera: Yes, but she kept her honor.

AL Vito: Awesome. 'Cause, you know, you can't protect them forever. Good for Linda.

A Corleone doesn't actively listen. When you "actively listen," you are immediately sending the message that you're a phony and a self-aggrandizer, knowledge that gives your adversary an edge. You may very well *be* a phony, but you want to hide that, don't you? Mmm, hmm.

* * *

5. Allies, Rivals, or Traitors (Oh, My)

WE'VE SPENT CHAPTERS 1-4 GETTING INTO A VITO STATE OF MIND—QUIET COMMUNICATION, SEPARATION OF BUSINESS AND PERSONAL ISSUES. Now it's time to use that new mindset to redefine how we see the business world, including how we see ourselves in it. It's time for our Corleone baptism. Once we dip into these unholy waters, though, the business world is never going to look the same again.

First, a bit of bad news: **You have no friends in the workplace.** And it's not just you—it's each one of us. It's not a reflection of your weight, your lisp, or your teeth. It's the nature of work. Business and true friendship do not mix.

That might be tough pill for some to swallow. The Corleones understood the true nature of business relationships. Business relationships are formed to facilitate the exchange of money. The nature of those relationships, hostile or somewhat amicable, depends on the level of competition and the depth of the mutual self-interests.

The Corleones could not do what they did for a living if they thought they were dealing with friends. Michael and Tom could execute a Tessio but would Mary Richards and Lou Grant ever execute Ted Baxter? Could Kirk and Spock ever push a button on Dr. McCoy?

5. Allies, Rivals, or Traitors (Oh, My)

You knew that you had some enemies, but you probably always thought that you had some friends in the office you could count on. So if you don't have friends, what do you have? You can classify all the people you have relationships with as **allies, rivals, or traitors.** This was how the Corleones viewed their business relationships. These three **meta-groupings** are all you need to classify and understand your relationships. Folksy, familiar terms like those listed below are truly meaningless:

- Male bonding/friendship terms like **buddy, chum,** and **pal**
- Terms of nationalistic identification like **amigo, compadre,** and **paisan**
- Sports derivatives like **go-to-guy, wingman, point-man,** and **quarterback**
- Animal nicknames like **tiger** or **big dog**
- Surfing friend terms like **dude, brother,** or the faux-Hawaiian "**bra**"
- Vague homilies like **good guy, nice guy, OK guy**
- Para-military terms of fellowship like **my man in the trenches, comrades, grunts,** or **troops**

You can and should still use these classifications with your work faux-friends (the people who were friends up until two minutes ago when you started this chapter). There's no benefit in giving them any insight into how you really view them and the other "dudes." Besides, a guy who thinks he's your best friend might be a little shocked or hurt to find out you regard him as an ally or rival.

In *The Godfather, Part II* (or GF2, for sake of abbreviation), Michael explained to Tom about the nature of their business family's loyalty: "**Their loyalty is based on money. Once you understand that you see that people are capable of practically anything.**"

Straight from Michael Corleone's mouth. If given more money or the promise of more money elsewhere, Michael's faithful henchmen could easily be bribed into taking action against him. Michael was especially astute and sensitive to this dynamic since he lacked his father's natural ability to engender affection. Michael was a bit of a stiff as the boss. To his credit, he knew it.

Losing Friends to Influence People

Divesting yourself of false friendship can be very empowering. Once you accept that your relationships at work are based purely on money, people become a lot easier to read and even predict. The friendship element adds perplexing dimensions when trying to interpret a person's actions.

Let's take a used car salesman, for example. We know they are trying to take the most money they can from us, so unless we're drunk or elderly, we don't buy into their efforts to befriend us. So, when you go with your mom to help her buy a used car and the salesman says, "Now, who is this lovely lady? Your sister?" or when he tells you that he just bought the exact car you're looking at for his own daughter, you know he's full of crap. He wants your money.

But what happens when one of our "friends" at work does something that obstructs or undermines us? It's confusing or unbelievable. We have trouble processing the information even if it's cut and dried.

"Why did Bob tell the customer that the new system wouldn't have any reporting capabilities? He knows better. Why would he do that?"

Why, indeed? Remove the pretense that Bob is a friend and, all of a sudden, a bunch of possible reasons materialize.

- He wants the project (and you) to fail.
- He wants to be a hero by "creating reports" that "don't exist."
- He wants to be the "guy with the real scoop" for the customer.
- He's too lazy to try to get the reports to work.

All seem perfectly reasonable actions of a **rival**. By reclassifying Bob as a rival, by removing the friendship tag, a slew of reasons can manifest themselves. But make him a friend again, and it's, "No. Not Bob. He'd never screw me like that." Yet this goes on every day in the workplace to millions of us.

In *The Godfather, Parts I and II*, the acceptance of false friends was the price of doing business. As events conspired to threaten the Corleone empire, they instantly realized that they had a traitor working in their midst. Mitigating the crisis depended on quick identification and elimination of the traitor. When they find him, whether it's Paulie, Carlo, or even Fredo, there's not a lot of hand wringing, just action. It was shocking to us when Michael killed Fredo, but then again we're not Corleones.

Not yet.

Cutting the Ties That Don't Bind

How do you sever these fake friendships? Emotionally, it's easy to do. Just wake up one day and do it—only do it in your head. Politically, there's benefit from your "friends" thinking that your relationship is still the same. In other words, don't do this:

> You: Hey, Bob. You got a second?
> Bob: What's up, compadre?
> You: I realized yesterday, after you screwed me by spreading false information about the system, that you weren't really my friend. Nobody is, but that's beside the point.
> Bob: But we're amigos! You're my *bra*, homey!
> You: No. After reading this really cool book, I realized that our friendship was based on false pretenses. We never really were friends.
> Bob: If that's how you feel, fine. I'm really hurt and confused, and I'll likely ally myself with your known rivals.
> You: You don't need to take this personally, Bob. You were never my friend. Like I said, according to this book, nobody really is.
> Bob: I'm going to devote my life to crushing you, you puny ant!

Did you see where and when that exchange went south? Keeping false friends in the dark about your new understanding is the best way to go. Go through the motions; attend the birthday parties and the happy hours, sign the goodbye cards, maintain the status quo. After all, that's probably all there was to the friendship in the first place. An occasional lunch. Toilet-papering someone's cube. Doesn't seem like all that much to lose, does it?

Remember that people act illogically. Although Bob was never your friend, he will likely hate the thought of losing you as one. It doesn't make sense. You don't have to understand people. Just to be able to predict their moves.

Allies, Rivals, and Traitors

Using Corleone-esque meta-groupings, your associates in the workplace break down into the following groups: **allies, rivals, and traitors.**

Starting with allies, our definition will be: "**someone whose self-interests coincide with yours, who will benefit from money exchanges that benefit you, and will share some information with you to facilitate that exchange.**" An ally:

- Is happy when you're happy (self-interests)
- Will share crucial information with you because it's in his/her self-interest
- Makes more money when you make more money

Some of the better-known Corleone allies were:

Godfather, Part I: Luca Brasi, Johnny Fontaine, Don Tommasino, Bonasera

Godfather, Part II: Cuban President Batista, Genco Abbandando, Al Niri, Rocco Lampone

Godfather, Part III: Don Tommasino (someone make this guy a family member already), Dominic Abbandando, B.J. Harrison

You'll note that the allies all have one thing in common. They're not very interesting. Loyalty, steadfastness, consistency, the qualities of good allies, do not make for great drama. This is the category most of your ex-friends will fall in. Allies are likely in the same department, share a few common enemies, work on projects together, or could be vendors/buyers for a critical system, where both reputations and careers depend on success. You both do well when your organization does well, although you may eventually compete for position and influence.

Sometimes allies work for you. Some are your managers. But now that you have them properly IDed, you can work more effectively with them. Don't change your personal style. If you're the nice guy, stay the nice guy. If you're the jerk, well, you have no intention of changing anyway.

As with friends, you will likely have some closer allies than others. Always remember that a close alliance only signifies more business interdependence, not friendship. Always keep your allies at arm's length emotionally and never become too dependent on them. It can create vulnerability, even when dealing with a strong alliance.

Tom Hagen and the Danger of Key Man Dependency

Tom was a Corleone ally who aspired to be a friend. No doubt Tom was an important part of their success. His interests were linked with theirs. He had a special skill set that most gangsters would love to have—a law degree. Tom made things happen for the Corleones, whereas Vito and Michael were idea guys. Tom was an advisor and implementer. He was the executor to their executive. However, Tom was the classic case of an employee who may have positioned himself as irreplaceable. It's a vulnerability inherent in close alliances.

For a while, Tom seemed like the only one getting any work done during GF1. Everything went through him, and Don Vito's rivals, most notably Sollozzo, picked up on it. This is known as a "key-man dependency." When you become too dependent on one ally, no matter how efficient he/she might be, it becomes a risk.

Remember, in GF1, that Sollozzo the Turk kidnapped Tom so that he could negotiate with Sonny through Tom. Tom was to be Sollozzo's agent. After the hit on Vito, Tom constantly urged Sonny to make a deal with Sollozzo. So, ask yourself, as the Corleones did, did Tom really have the Corleones' best interests in mind or his own?

With Vito down for the count and Sonny incapable of running the show, Michael sensed that Tom might have had too much influence and that Sonny may not have been capable of controlling him. So Michael took an interest in the business primarily to make sure that Sonny didn't blow it up before Vito got home.

Secondarily, though, Michael wanted to make sure that Tom didn't steal it from them. It's possible that Vito and Michael may have discussed this dependency, which resulted in Tom's demotion before the move to Vegas. With the famous line, "You're out, Tom," Michael marginalized Tom, while maybe firing a warning shot across his bow.

People have often read this moment as an unfair outcome for Tom. I remember a lot of "Awww, poor Tom" sentiment from my mom when we first watched it. But it was a smart move. Through deduction, Michael likely reasoned that Tom's interests might not have been as closely aligned to his family's, as they were pre-Sollozzo. Maybe Tom got tired of the last-minute California trips. Even if Michael was wrong, you can't fault him for tackling a key-man dependency.

By demoting Tom, he diminished the dependency on him as well. Now if anyone wanted to negotiate with the family, they would do it in the open and not try to undermine them through their staff.

When key men recognize a key-man dependency, they become your biggest headaches. You can and should solve your key-man problems immediately, either through elimination or delegation, no matter how much short-term pain it can cause.

History is rife with examples of how key men shot themselves in the foot within their organizations, and though the organizations suffered in the short term, long-term benefits were realized.

David Lee Roth and Van Halen, Shaquille O'Neal and the Lakers, Tom and the Corleones, Chevy Chase and *Saturday Night Live*—all of them overvalued their worth to their allies. All of them ended up either demoted or gone, while their organizations ultimately continued to flourish.

If you have a key-man ally, start thinking about finding a Sammy Hagar to replace him within the near future. If you are a key man, you may want to let your boss know that you recognize this as vulnerability. Ask your boss to throw some work to someone else. You don't want your boss thinking you think you are smarter than he/she is. Even though you are.

That is, unless you plan to betray him/her.

Business Empathy

Allies will be the closest thing to friends you have in the workplace. Alliances need to be nurtured or they can sour quickly. Just ask the United States and France about that. Buy a box of Girl Scout cookies from your allies occasionally or ask about the kids. Alliances also need to be **monitored**. Your allies will always be on the lookout for a better deal. They will always be more interested in their survival than yours.

But monitoring and nurturing won't do any good unless you can empathize with them. You should have a thorough understanding of what motivates, frightens, or stimulates them. This doesn't mean you sympathize. Empathy doesn't imply a warm, fuzzy feeling.

You can create a quick empathy checklist for each ally with some questions you should be able to answer with some certainty. Keep it in a password protected file on your desk and update it often. Your ability to manipulate and read people will determine your longevity in any job. So make it a regular task.

EMPATHY CHECKLIST for Bob

1. How is his/her mood? *Seems nervous lately*
2. What does Bob want? *Promotion. He's not shy about hinting.*
3. What does he think I want? *He probably thinks I like taking all the credit.*
4. Who are his potential allies? *Sylvia, Christine, and Steve*
5. What value does he have for me? *Bob can't keep secrets, and I can make him think anything at the drop of a hat. He is also good with the customers.*

An example of the dangers from not having any empathy happened to a friend of mine who was a credit analyst at one of the world's largest banks. He considered his manager a good friend, but my friend became concerned that there wasn't much work coming his way. Did his boss, his friend, not trust him?

The manager assured him that their relationship was as strong as ever. Safe as houses in fact. "Hang in there," the manager said. This was a slowdown related to the mortgage industry downturn. Everyone was looking for stuff to do. The credit analyst expressed concern that the lack of activity would expose him to a layoff. The manager said that he was concerned about being laid off himself.

"We're all in the soup together," the manager said.

I advised my friend to put himself in the manager's mind-set (empathize) and to stop thinking about the manager as a "friend." He put his feelings aside and did some investigating. He soon found out that the manager was intercepting his work and doing it himself. He was ensuring his own job security by jeopardizing his "friend's." They may have all been in the soup together, but the manager was the spoon and the credit analyst was the noodles.

If the credit analyst had been able to empathize, he would have seen this development coming months before. He could have floated his résumé around. He could have let it be known to other department heads that he had some bandwidth. But, unfortunately, it was too late for him to crawl out of the soup. My friend was laid off six months later. His boss friend? Promoted.

5. Allies, Rivals, or Traitors (Oh, My)

Minestrone Soup for The Soul: Empathy
Empathy with a Loose Nut

At a major consulting firm, Jack was brought in to tighten up the compliance reporting group. He came highly recommended as an experienced mentor-type, one who could mold the eager, but inexperienced and overwhelmed group into a productive, functional unit.

The group's de facto leader was an over eager, highly ambitious, but less than intelligent young lady who resented the fact that Jack was being brought in to be a true leader. She made it her personal business to undermine him. When Jack introduced new ways of working, she would whisper throughout the organization that he didn't understand their work. When he tried to be friendly, she would paint it as phoniness. When he worked close to the group, she would hold extended conversations in her native Russian tongue to fellow ex-pats. Jack sensed the conversation was about him.

Jack knew he had a problem. But he was also the new kid in town. She was the established ward bully. He needed her gone, but he knew that firing her was going to be difficult. Although she was stupid and bad at her job, she would regularly put in twelve- to fourteen-hour days. Jack knew the long hours were due to her incompetence, but people were sympathetic and thought she was a hero.

Jack lost many nights of sleep. She was incompetent. She was gossipy. She was dangerous. Why didn't anyone see it? He thought he might have to quit, so strong was her psychotic stranglehold on the group. Then one day, the quietest member of the team told Jack that she had felt harassed and bullied by the nut job. Now, she was making other people miserable. Jack felt that he needed to step up and do something. But what?

Jack employed his talent for empathy. He empathized with the kook. What kind of person was this bullying nut job?

Well, she was a bullying nut job, for one. Check. Paranoid. Jealous. Suspicious. Egotistical. Jack decided he would use her ego against her. He called a meeting with the harpy and told her he was very impressed with her work ethic. He told her he thought she could one day do his job. Knowing that she already believed this, he elaborated that he thought she should get advanced training in programming and business theory. He wanted her to pick out classes. He would gladly approve them all. The gorgon was flattered to the point of giddiness. She thanked Jack for finally recognizing what no one else had: that she was gifted. She signed up and took class after class. With the Queen of the Damned out of the office, Jack sprung into action. He established relationships with the group, free from her undermining gossip. The rest of the group found that he wasn't incompetent and wasn't a phony. They started to trust and rely on him. The group's customers found that dealing with Jack was a breath of fresh air. Here was someone with experience who could actually answer questions and produce.

When she returned from her classes, she was vexed to find that she had lost the psychic control of the group. She resumed her gossip attacks, but, this time, they fell on skeptical ears. The old man wasn't so bad, she was told. She seethed over the easy, breezy, casual relationship Jack now had with the team.

She was losing her grip. Now her ego would provide opportunity for Jack to go for the jugular. She requested a meeting, expressing concern that her role was diminished. She demanded more responsibilities. She was the de facto leader, she said—she was the one who worked all the long hours, and now wanted to be recognized and paid like a real leader.

Jack agreed that she was being underutilized. He agreed that she had leadership skills. He agreed that she should be managing her own group somewhere. Perhaps, he said, she had outgrown this job. It was, he said, unfortunate but not uncommon for gifted, talented, and now

HIGHLY TRAINED employees to feel that way. As hard as it was to face, Jack said it looked like she had outgrown her job and helpfully suggested that she look at the internal job postings. He pointed out that, armed with her new skill set acquired through recent training classes, she should have no trouble filling a leadership role.

A few days later, the dragon announced that she was transferring. She had outgrown this puny role, she said, and was going to work for a manager who appreciated her skills and would groom her for leadership. Congratulations, Jack said, controlling an instinct to cheer, weep for joy, and plant V-J Day style kisses on strangers in the streets. He would miss her, but he knew that this day would come.

He knew indeed. Because by empathizing, and lying artfully, Jack was able to painlessly extract a walking, breathing toothache.

Rivals

A rival is **someone who you know or suspect has self-interests that conflict with yours, who will benefit when you struggle, who tries to limit or control your earning potential, and who will not readily share information.**

Rivals:
- Are happy when you're unhappy (self-interests)
- Will lie or keep secrets from you
- Want to make more money than you, or keep you from making any

Companies want you to think of "the competition" as rivals, but many of you are buried so deep in the corporate catacombs that you never see or consider external competition. All of your competition is internal—a subordinate who wants your job, an internal customer who blames you for everything, a vice president who praises you for being smart and then steals your ideas, a manager who keeps you idle to decrease your value come review or layoff time.

Examples of the best-known Corleone rivals are:

Godfather, Part I - Don Barzinni, Virgil (The Turk) Sollozzo, Captain McCluskey, Bruno Tattaglia, Mo Green

Godfather, Part II - Hyman Roth, Johnny Ola, Senator Pat Geary, Don Fanucci, Don Cicci

Godfather, Part III - Joey Zaza, the Vatican bankers, Don Luchessi

Go down that list of rivals and what do they all have in common? Similar outcomes: death by Corleone. The other thing this list of rivals has in common is that most took a shot at killing either Michael or Vito Corleone. Obviously, you can't kill your rivals, but **once you've identified rivals, you have to eliminate them because they are going to eliminate you.**

You have to convert them to allies, cripple them, or remove them. How you do that depends on where they sit with respect to you in your organization. Are they colleagues, employees, or managers?

Rivals Who Work for You—The "T.O." Model

Named for bewildering NFL wide-receiver Terrell Owens, who inevitably alienates his employers and ends up being released, the T.O. model should be a warning for those of you with an employee-rivalry situation. The warning is this: they usually end on a bad note.

1. **Conversion**: For rivals who are your employees, this is your first option. You sit them down and give them a heart-to-heart. You threaten them or you charm them. The choice is yours. Consistent with the T.O. model, this works for a short time only. The Corleones generally did not have rivals who worked for them. They had "traitors," secret "rivals" (see section called "Traitors"). There were very few employees who would have openly voiced their problems with working for the Corleones.

2. **Cripple Them**: Put them on useless work, or give them no work. Start passing some of the usual tasks to one of their rivals. Never try any employee "discipline" or HR intercession. HR's first recommendation is always a written warning, the equivalent of a U.N. sanction in terms of ineffectiveness in containing problems. Written warnings backfire because they turn a rival into a martyr. Besides, you never want to let the employee know that you need help handling him.

3. **Elimination**: Here's a little-utilized technique that can save you time and money, eliminate any potential HR headache, and is actually a good use of HR. **Have HR monitor your employee-rival's computer use.** Do it for at least thirty days. Chances are you will find something irrefutable you can use to fire your employee-rival. Somewhere in that file, you'll find:

a. An email or instant message string that calls you fat, stupid, or dumb

b. Exorbitant amounts of time on a non-work-related Web sites

c. An email or instant message with improper language, harassment implications, or other behaviors that are in conflict with "core company values"

d. A trail that shows the employee is applying for jobs outside the company (This can be construed as "using company resources to conduct outside business.")

The beauty of this is you have a paper trail and HR created it for you. Traditionally, HR counsels **you** to create a paper trail. With HR having dug up the evidence, they will support your termination recommendation. Most Fortune 500 IT and HR departments have this capacity. I strongly suggest you use it, especially when dealing with a disruptive employee-rival.

Note: All employee-rivals start out as employee-allies. Using "empathy," as previously discussed, might help you lessen their chances of becoming "T.O.s." If you were paying attention to their decline, you may have spotted it sooner and saved everyone some real pain. So, no matter how much of a nut your employee-rival is, in reality, you have some measure of blame for his/her decline.

Rivals Who Don't Work for You

The Corleone method for dealing with serious rivals was to cut short their lives. You generally can't eliminate internal rivals who don't work for you. But here is a three-point program for controlling the damage they can do.

1. **Identification:** Vito knew he had a rival somewhere in the five families besides Tattaglia. So he used the Five-Family Summit to ferret him out (Don Barzinni). If you have a rival, call some meetings. Wait for someone to speak out or consistently challenge your ideas. Bingo! Rival spotted.

2. **Monitor:** Once you know who your rival is, use your allies to help monitor him/her. Chances are they are mutual rivals. If he takes a meeting with an ally, find out why. Watch how he/she interacts with his/her employees. You may be able to find an ally on that team.

3. **Mitigation:** Having a rival who doesn't work for you in corporate America means fighting a war of ideas. Your ideas versus his. Your methods versus his. Your job versus his. You must "win the hearts and minds" of the "undecideds." You know who your allies are. You know who his are. You know who the neutrals are. You have to convince the neutrals to bet on you rather than your rival.

Some techniques to win over undecideds are:

- **Bribery:** Buy lunches, Girl Scout cookies, drinks, etc., for the undecideds.
- **Vicious Nicknames:** This is not a technique I was particularly proud of and it also becomes a double-edged sword. The undecideds begin to wonder what secret nicknames you have for them. When you

resort to this, you are playing off of people's mob mentality and instincts for bullying. You are bringing out more ugliness in a group of people who are pretty ugly to begin with: corporate people.

- **Manage the Undecideds:** Give the undecideds superior service and deliverables while ignoring your rival's delivery needs. You'll win the undecideds over, and they will go to bat for you occasionally against your rivals. Soon you'll have undecideds saying things like, "Gee. Your work is great. I can't understand why Janine thinks you're an idiot."

Minestrone Soup for the Soul: Vicious Nicknames
Val Trumps Ratonzel

Val was having the toughest time with Cindy. Cindy was a difficult internal client, to say the least, the toughest in the company. She was demanding, yet disorganized. She was bossy, yet accepted no responsibility for failures. And she was an email demon. Every morning there were seven or eight complaining emails waiting for Val from her nemesis. What's worse, Cindy always copied Val's boss and her boss.

The pressure was on Val. She was capable of meeting realistic expectations, but Cindy was just too demanding. Val also knew that to play the "too demanding card" would imply that Cindy was working harder than her, or that Val couldn't keep up.

What Val had figured out was that Cindy was using her as an excuse not to perform. While Val was furiously generating data for Cindy's group, Cindy would summarily reject it. When Cindy was called to the carpet for sloppy work, she would always blame Val and pull out the numerous emails where she documented "problems."

Everyone knew Cindy was difficult, but they thought it was productive perfectionism. Cindy was prickly to everyone, but they put up with it because she seemed to be on top of everything.

Val needed to do something—something drastic, something harsh. It wasn't a personal decision. It was business. Cindy was an immovable object on Val's path to success. Cindy was a very large woman, with long blonde hair that reached down to her buttocks. Val decided to play the vicious nickname card. One day in a meeting with her team, Val referred to Cindy as "Ratonzel" as in "Rapunzel, Rapunzel, let down your hair." The team cracked up. People like gossip and drama. Some became curious. The nosy ones questioned Val about Cindy. Val suddenly had a forum. Soon she also had supporters.

It was a vicious, classless move, Val thought, but no more classless than Cindy falsely blaming her for all her troubles and failures. Cindy's tactic could have cost Val come review time. And all Val did was make fun of her hair. Meow.

People started to see through Cindy's shenanigans and sympathized with Val. A senior supportive manager was brought in to run point for Val, and he recognized that she was delivering, despite what Cindy claimed.

An understanding was reached and, eventually, Val earned a promotion and some more challenging work. And it may have been a coincidence, but, later that year, Cindy got a haircut.

Michael Corleone's key rival in GF2 was Hyman Roth, and his plan to contain him had the key elements of this program.

1. **Identification:** Michael knew Hyman was a rival, but who else was? How far did Hyman's influence reach?

2. **Monitor:** He needed to monitor "first hand" what Hyman was up to. So with events accelerating, Michael caught the next train to Miami.
3. **Mitigation:** Michael killed Hyman. Obviously, that choice is closed to us, but giving Hyman the nickname "Stumpy" was not an option that would have worked for Michael.

Traitors

Our definition of traitor is **a former ally whose self-interests have come in direct conflict with yours, yet he continues to position himself as an ally, while engaging your rivals.** Traitors are like termites; you don't know you have them until the damage is done.

Traitors can drive you crazy if you have one, and crazy if you don't. Imagining you have a traitor can be almost as divisive to your team as having one. Traitors are not unlike exotic flu outbreaks in that the worry about the disease is sometimes worse than the actual symptoms. True traitors are relatively rare occurrences because:

- Being a traitor is stressful to the traitor. Most traitors are incapable of sustaining the stress (see Leonardo DiCaprio in *The Departed*).
- Nobody likes being thought of as a traitor. People would rather quit than betray even the most idiotic or petty manager. Traitors carry a stigma—Judas, Benedict Arnold, Fredo, Jon of *Jon and Kate Plus 8*. To the world at large, they are the lowest of the low. As a result of the stigma, most traitors just sort of toy with the idea in their heads.

Typical candidates for traitors are:

- Long-time employees who've never been promoted and have made their displeasure known. They seek to close the gap between you and themselves. This was Fredo's motive for jumping teams.
- An employee who thinks he or she is the real brains in your group—a "key-man" type.
- Managers who feel like they are on the hot seat. Some managers will vent to you about their troubles in an attempt to win your sympathy and loyalty. Meanwhile, they are figuring out ways to blame their screw-ups on you.

Traitors from the Godfather Saga include:

> *The Godfather, Part I*— Tessio, Carlo, Fabrizzio
> *The Godfather II*—Fredo Corleone
> *The Godfather Part III*—Don Altobello

Finding / Dealing with Traitors

The identification of your traitor will test your "It's Not Personal" mettle like nothing else will. That's because a traitor is by necessity an ex-ally (and, in Fredo's case, a brother and soon-to-be ex-person), and if your "It's Not Personal" muscle isn't fully developed, there could be feelings involved in the elimination steps.

Remember to distance yourself always. Removal of a traitor is not a choice. Like removing a cockroach from your kitchen table, it's a no-brainer and an emotionless act. The tough part is actually making the call on whether he's a traitor or not.

Spotting a traitor is not easy. Watch Michael in the Havana café scene, enjoying a cocktail with Fredo. He knows there is something wrong with Fredo (big news flash there), but he quickly shakes it out of his head. Fredo was twitchy and nervous when discussing Hyman Roth, twitchy even for Fredo. Michael picked up on it but dismissed it.

It's tough to make the call, and emotion can blind the best of us. It was only after Fredo's slip-up in the burlesque club (watching *Superman*) that Michael was sure, and even then he was shocked.

The Michael-Fredo dynamic points out a universal truth about betrayal: It's easier to prevent someone from becoming a traitor than to later prove that they are one. So here are some tips and examples on how to spot a potential traitor before it's too late. Traitor prevention is a lot like the concept of wellness. A little prevention now can avert a lot of pain later.

1. **The "Tessio" Model: The smart, under-appreciated one.** The Tessio archetype is typically extremely smart, an established and respected veteran, and yet likely feels under-appreciated or undercompensated. Try to convert the Tessio before he goes over the wall. Remember to flatter and compensate that Tessio. Figure out a promotion path that will keep him happy for a while. A well-rewarded Tessio is a happy Tessio. If your Tessio is an ally that doesn't work for you but may resent your success, make sure you flatter and credit him in emails and meetings.

2. **The "Fredo" Model: The dumb, under-appreciated one.** Your dumb, unappreciated

types are more likely to go over the walls, since they haven't really thought out the consequences. As with your Tessio, if you suspect a potential problem with your stupid ally, try to head it off before it becomes betrayal. Limit your Fredo's exposure to your rivals. Since he is stupid, your rivals can more easily buy him off. As an added bonus, you won't have to hear him drone on and stammer at meetings anymore.

The upside of eliminating your dumb, under-appreciated employee is that you are likely losing someone who hasn't pulled his weight in years, as opposed to a Tessio, who was productive, despite starting to look uncannily like Abe Vigoda in his later years.

Fredo (John Cazale) and Michael (Al Pacino) in an eerie shot that appears to be an homage to Iago and Othello. It also looks a little like a Loggins and Messina album cover.

For the casual viewer of *Godfather, Part II* (and is there really such a thing?), it may be of interest to note the Shakespearean undertones and allusions in the Michael and Fredo relationship.

Watch the Havana café scene where Michael confides in Fredo, and Fredo nearly spills his guts. In this scene, I can't help think of Shakespeare's *Othello*, with Michael as the troubled monarch and Fredo as his treacherous vizier, Iago. In the play *Othello*, Iago claims to have been unfairly passed over for promotion by *"**Michael Cassio.**"* Were Coppola and Puzo paying homage to Shakespeare's classic play of power and betrayal? Did he just need them to scootch a little closer? Who knows? To me it seems obvious, especially when looking at the image above.

Somewhere around your sixth or seventh viewing of either movie, these symbols start to become more apparent. But beware: By the time you find yourself writing books about the *Godfather* saga, you see images everywhere and will rightly question your sanity. For example, when I'm tired, I see Clemenza's giant saucepot as a metaphor for the "blood of Christ." For more about these symbols, see the final chapter, "**The DaVito Code**," which interprets (or sometimes makes up) some of the more compelling symbolism employed in the saga.

3. **The "Don Altobello" Model: The Old, Arrogant One.** Altobellos are usually very senior in years, but not position. They like to make life miserable for their young pup colleagues. They like to show they still have a few teeth in their old head, tethered however loosely with DentuCream. You should keep an especially close eye on Altobellos in customer-facing positions. They may not be interested in supplanting or removing you, but they

like to tell customers things like, "That's not how I would have done it, but, hey, what do I know? I've only been here fifteen years."

4. **The "Fabrizzio/Carlo/Paulie" Model: Young, Stupid, and Ambitious.** Watch out for newer, younger members with poor work habits. These are guys who think that there's an elevator to the top instead of a staircase. Typically, they spend most of their day calculating the most BMW that they can afford on their salaries instead of working. Keep an ear open for conversations that begin with, "Man, what I could do with his money." Every organization has a "Carlo" on their team. He reeks of Axe body-wash and spray, works out religiously, and manages to drop workout references into every conversation, as in, "I was working on my lats today when I got an idea for the proposal." He flirts with every admin and sees the world as divided into two categories: "old guys" and "him." Which means he sees you as an "old guy." A fat cat—an overpaid fat cat who is in his way.

   Be firm and authoritative if you suspect you are dealing with one. Carlos/Paulie-type traitors are the most likely to be indiscreet, so use your company's IT monitoring capacity to nail such a type, if it's in your purview. Also, since they are new, losing them will have the least negative impact on you and your team.

Turning Traitors into "Traitor-ade"

Betrayal is an expensive proposition but true to the spirit of the Corleones, you mustn't take it personally and you need to get over it quickly. There are some positives you can take out of dealing with a traitor. You want to send a message that the identification of the traitor points out your strength, not your weakness. Here's how you can turn traitors into traitor-ade. The trick here is to *act* like you are taking it personally.

1. **After firing your traitor, immediately promote the traitor's assistant**—This will tell your troops that loyalty is rewarded as swiftly as disloyalty is punished. You'd also be indirectly encouraging employees to ferret out traitors. It will also look like the traitor's assistant had something to do with his/her boss' demise. This system worked out great for the Soviets for years, leading to some of their longest, most famous purges.

2. **Quickly remove all traces of the traitor**—Clear out his desk. Take his name off all signage and documents. Get him wiped out of email. Leave a cryptic voice-mail message. After my layoff, anyone who called my extension received this ominous message: "The number you have reached is a non-working number. This phone does not accept voicemail messages." I always thought the phrase "non-working" number was interesting. You don't want to give anyone the time or opportunity to feel

nostalgic about him. The thoroughness with which you wipe out his legacy will send a chill up your employees' spines. Think "Sethi and Moses" from *The Ten Commandments.* ("Let the name Moses be stricken from every temple and obelisk!" BOOM!)

3. **Refuse to use the traitor's name**—Call him "that person" or "your predecessor." You won't be taking betrayal personally, of course—you'll just pretend to. Loyal employees will perceive you're hurt and will want to circle the wagons in support of you, and employees on the loyalty bubble will fear their own legacies being obliterated should they cross the line. And who knows? Some of the women working for you may find your new vulnerability sexy.

Minestrone Soup for the Soul: Dealing with Traitors
Pod-Cast Away

Mike's first taste of management at the call center was a rough one. Smart, hard working, and likeable, he found out the hard way that some people just don't like managers. One of them, Ed, was a particular jerk to him. He would glare at Mike when he said "good morning." Whenever Mike walked by the group, he noticed that everyone eyed Ed to catch a reaction. When he turned the corner and the group was out of view, he inevitably heard titters. Ed was the team's clown and he was poking fun at Mike. Mike knew it, but what could he do? A leader has to roll with the punches.

One day, on a trip to the vending machines, Mike offered to buy the team sodas. Ed piped up, "Thank you, Santa Claus." The team broke up in laughter—disproportionately, Mike thought. Of course,

Mike had a white beard, was bald, and had a potbelly. He put it together. Funny Ed, that funny, funny guy, had obviously coined the nickname "Santa Claus" for Mike. And since funny guys make their living out on the edge, Ed had thrown the inside joke right out there in Mike's face, for everyone's enjoyment. He calculated correctly that the group would admire his guts for the move.

However, he miscalculated Mike's sensitivity and self-awareness. Mike knew that he looked like Santa Claus and had learned over the years to live with the gentle tummy pokes and the occasional child jumping into his lap. But it still hurt to be ridiculed behind his back about it.

He could go one of two ways with this. He could acknowledge that he understood the joke, and openly go along with it. This might earn Ed's respect, but Mike thought that Ed, like other funny, funny guys, couldn't be trusted to let him off the hook. Establishing an understanding with Ed would've just given him more material for his fun funniness and the fact that Mike was friendly to him would only add to other people's enjoyment of Ed's scorn.

He had always suspected as much, but Ed now showed himself to be a traitor. He needed to be eliminated. Mike made up his mind to fire Ed. This wasn't personal. It was business. Ed wasn't a valuable employee. His work was average or below. And he was affecting Mike's concentration and ability to lead. That would undermine the group's mission. A firing would also send a chill up the spines of all Ed's fans.

But how to do it? He needed to be strong and vindictive, without appearing to be. Ed was not a great employee, but not a bad one, either. And his jokiness and contempt for authority made him popular with the group.

Mike decided to use HR's system-monitoring capabilities to monitor Ed's computer usage, email, and instant messages. He reasoned that a comedic genius like Ed's would definitely manifest itself in a paper trail. Sure enough, after three weeks of monitoring, Mike found enough insults about him and others to call Ed to the carpet.

But it wasn't enough. Firing Ed because he called him "Santa" might make Mike look petty and insecure. But studying the rest of the file, Mike found Ed's smoking gun. Internet usage reports showed that Ed spent most of his day on one particular Web site. It turned out that Ed owned a commercial Internet radio station and was managing the broadcasts while at work.

In a clear violation of improper usage rules, Ed was called into a meeting and presented with the overwhelming evidence. He would have to be terminated, Mike said. Ed gave Mike a slight nod of admiration that seemed to say, "You got me, you fat, Santa-looking S.O.B. Good for you."

Mike nodded back, shook his hand, and wished Ed well. He was sure that Ed would land on his feet, he said, and he wished Ed, "Good luck and a very merry Christmas."

* * *

6. WWVD: What Would Vito Do?

How many times have you been facing a problem when you said, "I don't know what to do"? The funny thing about that statement is that, given the same problem and circumstances, you'd probably be able to surmise with reasonable acuity what other people would do. Why is that? Why do we have so much trouble deciding for ourselves?

Who cares "why." The real trick is to take advantage of that knowledge of others.

Let's take a hypothetical situation. You are a lead underwriter at a mortgage company who gets paid a bonus based on how many files you close. You like your job. You're also a natural leader and excellent trainer. Your manager has offered you a role as a department head. More work, same pay, but its *management*. Exposure, leadership training, nice title bump, no more punching the clock.

It sounds great, but on the other hand, you're doing great as an underwriter. You are killing it with respect to your productivity bonus. You know your job "cold."

You face a tough call. You say to yourself, "I don't know what to do," as millions of us do every day. But let's play some word/personality association games. Here's a list of famous fictional and non-fiction characters—characters that all of us know from countless stories, episodes, cartoons, news articles, and so on. You may not necessarily like them. But you know them. What would *they* do given your position? In a few words, write down the decisions and justifications for taking or not taking the promotion as the following characters:

1. Fred Flintstone
2. Captain Kirk
3. Barack Obama
4. George W. Bush
5. Bugs Bunny
6. Gordon Gecko (*Wall Street*)
7. John Lennon
8. Paul McCartney
9. Gilligan
10. Annakin Skywalker

Here's my take on what these characters would do, given the promotion dilemma.

1. **Fred Flintstone** - He'd pass on the offer. He's happy to be a working slob.
2. **Captain James Kirk** - He wants to be a leader. He is not afraid of responsibility and sees it as his destiny to improve the lot of others.
3. **Young Barack Obama** – Same as Kirk
4. **Young George W. Bush** - He hated authority and saw himself as a manager/leader. He'd take the promotion.
5. **Bugs Bunny** – Despite his intelligence and natural leadership ability, Bugs is a libertarian. Happy to live and let live. He enjoys the simple things in life.

Some carrots, a nice, clean hole. Promotion and title would hold little allure to him. Bugs would pass.

6. **Gordon Gecko (*Wall Street*)** - Money and independence were his goals. He'd take whichever job paid more money short-term, likely the lead underwriter position. Gordon's goal was to make it on his own, not as a manger for a corporation.

7. **John Lennon** - He'd pass. "A Working Class Hero is something to be." Coming from a working-class background, John had a bit of a socialist, populist bent to him. He wouldn't enjoy managing others and, in the later Beatles years, seemed to defer a lot of the leadership role to Paul.

8. **Paul McCartney** - He'd take it. Paul was and still is aggressively ambitious. He's still out there making albums, still determined to show he's a kingpin in pop music. In the later Beatle years, it was Paul who drove them to form Apple Records, Corp.

9. **Gilligan** – Gilligan, unlike most stupid people, knew his limitations. He would have passed on the promotion, unless this were an episode where he was hit on the head with a coconut and underwent some kind of temporary transformation into a leadership type—complete with moustache and monocle.

10. **Annakin Skywalker** – Annakin's dark side revolved around recognition and ambition. He'd take it in a heartbeat, despite Yoda's misgivings about his being offered the job. The more responsibility Annakin got, the more exposed he got to corrupting influences like Chancellor Palpatine.

6. WWVD: What Would Vito Do?

We can compare answers but the real point is that you probably didn't take longer than a few minutes to decide. You have enough familiarity with the characters and seen them in enough situations to predict with some certainty what they'd do.

The Character of You

"You" are the character you've been playing your whole life, yet a lot of us still can't figure out what we're supposed to do. We fumble our lines, miss our marks and don't understand our motivations. Oftentimes, we don't react or decide naturally, according to our instincts or best interests. We might do what Mom and Dad would approve of, do what's best for family, or do what seems safest or most practical.

Because we have conflicting interests (our own instinctive ones versus our responsibilities or inner voices), we have trouble making decisions. Yet when we put ourselves in another person's shoes, we have no trouble making decisions. How many of us give great advice to friends yet have trouble managing our own lives?

Most of us have no idea what the character of "You" would do without a lot of hand wringing. Yet we have a fair idea what a famous character like Fred Mertz, Hawkeye Pierce or Donald Trump would do. Why not use our knowledge of other characters to drive our decisions, especially if they are successful? And if Vito Corleone is our business standard bearer, why not take advantage of our knowledge of him? Let's make Vito's personality and decision-making a reality check for our decision-making process and we should end up with similar outcomes.

"What Would Vito Do?" Test

Let's do that same kind of test, this time using only Vito as our decision-maker, and using variable situations.

1. Coke or Pepsi?
2. Paper or plastic?
3. Regular or premium at the pump?
4. McCain or Obama?
5. The Beatles or The Rolling Stones?
6. Frank Sinatra or Dean Martin?
7. Dining in or eating out?
8. Shower or bath?
9. Red wine or white?
10. Chinese take-out or Mexican?

Here are my responses using my Vito proxy:

1. **Coke or Pepsi?** Coke. Vito wouldn't identify with Pepsi's hip image and would trust the time-tested Coke formula, even if it is secret.
2. **Paper or plastic?** Paper. Vito wouldn't trust new-fangled plastic.
3. **Regular or premium at the pump?** Regular. Vito came from real poverty. No matter how rich they get, these types of people never forget the value of money.
4. **McCain or Obama?** I believe Obama. Vito would not like a federal government that legislates morality which is frequently part of the G.O.P platform. Coming from extreme poverty, Vito was also a

populist. Despite being filthy rich, he would always feel emotional ties to the lower- and middle-classes.

5.   **The Beatles or The Rolling Stones?** The Beatles. I believe Vito would have liked the pleasant, accessible escapist quality of The Beatles over the grittier, more sexually overt Stones.

6.   **Frank Sinatra or Dean Martin?** Sinatra. Vito would not have approved of Dino's overt playboy persona. Although Sinatra was as big a playboy as Dino pretended to be, Vito would have appreciated Frank's discretion.

7.   **Dining in or eating out?** Dine in. More family time.

8.   **Shower or bath?** Shower. Who's got time for a bath? This man had a business to run.

9.   **Red wine or white?** Red. Goes better with sauce. You can just open it and pour and not wait for it to chill. Red wine also has alkaloids and anti-oxidants and although these weren't discovered at the time, for thousands of years Italians knew red wine to be "good for you."

10.   **Chinese take-out or Mexican?** Since the boys and the capos were eating Chinese take-out in a scene from GF1, that's where I'm leaning.

Introducing WWVD—What Would Vito Do?

How close did we get? I bet we're within two or three answers. So given your familiarity with the character, and given Vito Corleone's track record for success, why wouldn't you use him as a sounding board for all your ideas or tough calls? Next time you're faced with a critical decision, ask yourself, "What Would Vito Do?"

If you ask yourself the question at critical times and then answer it honestly, putting yourself in Vito's skin, you should be able to predict accurately what Vito would do. If you've seen *The Godfather* more than three times, you have a pretty good feel for WWVD. Your understanding of Vito's personality gives you enough to apply WWVD effectively.

How Can WWVD Help You Every Day?

Throughout mankind's history, we've learned from the examples of great men before us: philosophers, prophets, strategists, presidents, and Bono. Although none of us are ever likely to declare war or save or topple a government, we still look to them for guidance. Similarly, Vito Corleone faced greater responsibilities than we ever will. But as with the great men of the past, don't let Vito Corleone's "distance" from us in terms of workload or influence dissuade you from using his example. Don't let the fact that he's fictional put you off, either.

While you may not ever have the types of leadership or life and death decisions Vito must face, WWVD can still help you at times. It can certainly prevent you from making stupid mistakes in your life. Can you imagine Vito buying a car when he couldn't afford it or dropping out of college to climb K-2?

Let's apply some good, old-fashioned WWVD to some common scenarios:

1. **New girl at the office shows an interest in becoming better friends with you. WWVD?** Nip

it in the bud. Vito never mixed work with pleasure (see chapter 1). But if you have to have a girl tonight, that's what Craigslist is for. And if you have a girl waiting for you at home, you definitely know what Vito would do.

2. **You're the new guy and you sense the legacy gang might be talking behind your back.** WWVD? Be patient and do nothing. You're not in a position of strength yet. Don't take it personally. Isolating the new guy is primitive, typical tribal behavior, and would happen to whichever new guy walked in the door. Vito wouldn't react at all, leaving the gossiper(s) to find more interesting, reactive targets. Later, after you've moved up the ladder and eventually this person comes under your protection, then you can crush him like the slug he/she is.

3. **Your boss seems to take a lot of pleasure in pointing out your mistakes.** Your boss is Don Fanucci, threatened by you, but masking it by bullying you. Maybe he does think you're an idiot. Is he starting a war of attrition, hoping you'll eventually quit? Does he feel under the gun? WWVD? In this situation, there are a lot of questions that need answering, so my hunch is that Vito would get some answers. This is reconnaissance time. He'd cast around, learning more about his boss' standing, sifting through some rumors, making sure he has all the facts.

Maybe the biggest benefit of a WWVD-type method is that it makes you sit down and analyze a problem objectively.

Instead of worrying about a problem, you're always chipping away at it. Thinking about it instead of avoiding it. *Wearing the problem down instead of vice versa.*

What Would Young Vito vs. Old Vito Do?

Since you likely aren't a CEO or head of state, you are at a stage in your career where you are at the level of a young Vito— just starting out, or banging up against the glass ceiling like Vito was at the Abbandando groceries. A lot of your WWVD choices at this stage will involve patience and opportunism. These aren't as sexy as the old Vito choices—assassination, threats, and assault. There were a lot more options for direct action for old Vito as there will be for you as you move up the ladder.

But while you're in the start-up or stalled phase of your career, be patient like young Vito. Likely, a lot of your WWVD choices will involve waiting for the right moment to strike. If your eyes are always looking for opportunities, you'll spot them more easily, much in the same way that you start noticing Hybrids on the road once you've made a down payment. He may not come along often, but, once in a while, a fat, lazy, and clownish Don Fanucci, or, in other words, Don Opportunity is going to wander into your life. He's a cash cow just waiting for someone with the brains and guts to slaughter him. Be patient, "young Vito," your time will come. Have your revolver and towel ready for when it does. In the meantime, let Vito be your guide for the tougher day-to-day decisions you have to face.

* * *

6. WWVD: What Would Vito Do?

Minestrone Soup for the Soul: What Would Vito Do?
Tom's Classy End Game

  Tom was on disability leave when he got the word: He had been transferred to a new group…a new boss…a new location. He had expected this. It was the middle of the recession and financial services companies like his were in tumult. He expected to be laid off, but this transfer was not welcome news.

  Tom had heard that his new boss was clinically crazy. She was visibly nervous, self-centered in conversation, egomaniacal, and had a peculiar habit of wearing lipstick around her lips instead of on them. He knew deep down that this was a very bad development for him. His return from disability date was coming up. To compound matters, Tom didn't feel fully recovered from his accident that caused the disability in the first place. He would be dealing with physical pain at a time when he needed to be at his best.

  When he returned to work to meet his crazy new boss, his fears were realized. He found Elena to be manipulative, egotistical, and gossipy, with those strangely glossed lips giving her, at best, an off-putting, Fellini-esque appearance. At worst, her red-smeared maw made her seem bloodthirsty or devilish. In their first meeting, she denigrated her former team members, pointed out how stupid she thought everyone around her was, while managing to speak twenty minutes to Tom without a nanosecond's worth of eye contact with him. Tom took a deep breath and tried to smile through all the craziness, but every self-aggrandizing and unkind word made him apprehensive.

  Tom was in a fight for his life. He decided to give it his very best shot. If the crazy lady was going to be his boss, then he was going to do his best to win her over.

  There was trouble right out of the gates. Their skill sets didn't mesh, since Tom was more of a technical resource and Elena an insurance whiz. They had trouble communicating with each other. Whenever Tom questioned Elena about a task she gave him, she reacted like it was a personal challenge, whereas Tom saw this as normal discovery and discourse. Whenever Tom came to Elena with a problem, the first words out of her mouth were, "Not that I don't believe you, but…."

Typical of a liar, Tom thought. She thinks everyone around her is constantly lying. Sometimes she was visibly agitated around Tom, as if the very act of talking to him was inconvenient and beneath her. The more Tom tried to be agreeable, the more contempt she seemed to have for him. The combination of Elena's hostility and her dishonesty began to make Tom nervous. If she is constantly running down other people, he thought, God knows what she must be saying about me. This tension, coupled with his physical discomfort, began to manifest itself in anxiety symptoms such as insomnia, tremors, and hot flashes.

Proximity to Elena only made the issue worse. She was the type of person Tom just couldn't connect with. She spoke in long, redundant stanzas, turning every conversation into a monologue about how much smarter she was than everyone else. She was adverse to eye contact, or, rather, she was disinterested in it, since the images in her head were much more interesting to her than Tom, the feckless employee she was saddled with. She also spoke with an affected urbanity, a Lauren Bacall-esque charm school phoniness that accented her self-importance. She had a personality that down-to-earth Tom couldn't stomach.

Things came to a head that first week over a report that Tom was working on for her. Elena pointed out some genuine concerns with the work, and Tom responded instantly and thoroughly to correct them. When he resubmitted the report, Elena said that it was worse than before and questioned whether Tom had the capacity to do this job. He had been with the company for five years and no one had ever said anything like that. This made Tom panic. But he focused enough to discover an error in Elena's reconciliation. His report did in fact balance to the ledger. When he pointed it out to her, she was furious and threw him out of her office. Tom mustered up enough nerve to call Elena "intellectually dishonest" to her face.

This was all within the first week. Tom knew Elena was railroading him. He thought about going to her boss, but he knew her boss would side with her and that would just make things worse. He knew Elena was going to terminate him, but he didn't want to get tossed out in the street. He had two kids and was his family's sole provider. And he was still physically sick and in pain.

Tom reasoned that there would be no working with Elena. Every word out of her bizarrely painted mouth was like a body blow for him. So he applied for a transfer. He knew that he wasn't eligible, that there were no open positions, and that this would expose him to Elena and her boss. He needed protection, but he didn't want to antagonize a lunatic. A transfer would put him on HR's radar without incriminating Elena. But it still wouldn't protect him from her. After looking at all factors, he figured that the best he could do in this environment would be a layoff. Having five years under his belt, he knew exactly what his severance benefits were. But he needed to diffuse the landmines that Elena kept heaving at him so that he could survive to the next rounds of layoffs.

*Taking a page from Vito's book, Tom knew his only play was to control his own reactions to Elena's lunacy. He began to think about how Vito would react in situations like this. What would Vito do? What **could** Vito do when faced with a crazy person?*

Vito would never let anyone see him sweat. As Tom imagined Vito's cool under fire, sure enough it began to calm him. Whenever Elena came into his cubicle, Tom would be able to control his territory and keep his cool in the face of her lying.

Things calmed down internally for Tom. He was at peace, resigned to his fate, as the image of Vito gave him the strength to cope. Elena kept hammering at him with criticism, suspicion, and contempt, but Tom handled it all with the dignity of a pontiff and when things got really rough, a fake limp. Friends and co-workers who had squirmed at his plight began to express their admiration for his strength. He would smile and say, "Graci" and return to his cubicle, awaiting his walking papers. Eventually, Elena came to a grudging détente with Tom. She was no longer antagonistic. She even managed to be professional to him at times.

His number finally came up right around his fifth anniversary with the company. Elena called him into a meeting room. Tom knew what was coming and when he saw the beefy, purplish HR adjutant in the room, he knew the end was here. He excused himself for a moment to collect himself. He went to the restroom, splashed a little water on his face, and took a moment to stifle the emotions welling up inside of him. It was a miserable few weeks, and the emotions he was suppressing were those of relief, not anxiety. As Little Alex said when leaving his prison in A Clockwork Orange, *"You're always a malenky bit sad to leave a place you've spent a lot of time in, no matter how awful it was." Tom was indeed, a malenky bit sad.*

He collected himself, straightened his clothes, and went in with a mental picture of young Vito graciously accepting his firing from the grocery store. He would face his end with the same quiet calm and absence of regret. He'd deprive Elena of any satisfaction though she tried hard to push his buttons at the exit interview, pointedly asking for his keys and telling HR to walk Tom to the door, implying he might fake a fall on a banana peel.

In the end, Elena won the battle, but Tom minimized the damage. He had turned a near firing into a seventeen-week layoff package with a rehire status. He'd relax, get better, rest, and maybe, just maybe, write that book that he'd been kicking around in his head for years. Maybe

6. WWVD: What Would Vito Do?

it would be a self-help book about how to deal with people like Elena. Maybe he would use her first name, so she would know....

It was a tough few weeks, but with his understanding of what Vito would do, he had learned to tap an inner strength that he didn't think he had. Elena, meanwhile, would look for fresh victims to unleash her demons on and continue her slow descent into madness. Then, one day, Tom hoped, she would die a lonely, painful death, her bitterness and nastiness having precluded her from having any family by her side, her face twisted in a garish expression of fright and pain as if the rottenness in her soul were transcribing itself indelibly on her features. Dead and alone, she'd receive the final insult when her morticians, trying to make her look her best, put her lipstick directly on her lips, instead of outside them.

* * *

7. My Corleone Has a First Name—It's S-O-N-N-Y: Your Inner Corleone

WHEN I FIRST SAW *THE GODFATHER*, THERE WAS ONE CHARACTER BESIDES VITO THAT COMPLETELY HOOKED ME. That was Santino ("Sonny") Corleone. Good-looking, broad-shouldered, quick-witted, magnetic, and fiercely protective of his family, Sonny was everything that I wasn't. Apparently, even in movies, opposites attract.

The strong ensemble of the Godfather Saga offered audiences a choice of characters that they could connect with. My father, with his thirty-five years as a warehouse supervisor, seemed to warm up to Tom Hagen. Tom was the "working man" of the Corleone family. Humble, soft-spoken, but as capable as any gangster who donned a fedora. My father, who worked in the same Lower East Side warehouse until retirement, and who enjoys robust physical and mental health into his eighties, must have connected with Tom's steadfast, hard-working, low-key, almost puritanical style.

Many of my Italian friends saw themselves as Michael. Michael was the model for second-generation Italians—in touch with his Italian roots, yet seamlessly integrated into American culture. He embodied financial success by any American standard with a Camelot-era air of elegance, while most of my friends who thought they were "Michaels" couldn't get through a calzone without spilling half of the contents on their laps.

We can decide like Vito using WWVD, but do we have the internal makings of a Vito Corleone? Or are we more like Michael—quiet, fearless, and ambitious? Are we Tom Hagens—efficient, determined, and ruthless? Or are we, God forbid, more like Fredo—fearful, resentful, lazy, and maybe a little dim?

It's time to discover which Corleone you are, and how to avoid the mistakes they made, while capitalizing on their strengths. Caution: Remember, these discussions are purely academic. It's important that whomever you identify with, you don't lock yourself into one character or tactic for the rest of your career. You may start out a Sonny, but your goal may be to be a Michael. You may be a stuffed ascot like Michael now, but your goal may be to loosen up and get more women, like Sonny.

You will be taking a test, designed to pinpoint which Corleone you tend to behave like. This does not mean that you are predestined to be "Tom" or "Michael." These results are *non-binding*. This will be a lot like those corporate orientation or team-building exercises, in which you take a quiz and someone tells you that you are a "builder," "creator," or "facilitator," then they send you back to your cubicle to a job that has nothing to do with building or creating. Here, our archetypes will have real names like "Fredo" or "Santino." Names we can identify with. Roles with *teeth!*

Corleone Top 25 Power Rankings

Let's start off with our power rankings for the top twenty-five "players" from the Godfather Saga (including rivals and traitors). Though the rest of this chapter deals with the core Corleones, a power ranking can give you an idea of what matters in the Corleone universe, who had it, and who didn't.

Corleone power rankings differ a little from traditional sports power rankings or *Fortune*'s "Most Influential" type lists. Whereas those lists focus on "who won" or "who earned" or "who influenced," in the Corleone universe, "how badly" you want something is almost as important as whether you achieved your goal or not. In our power rankings, we reward the effort almost as much as the outcome. On our list, there are such things as "good losers." With that in mind, let's get to the rankings.

1. **Vito Corleone:** The gold standard. Blessed with a once-in-a-generation blend of ruthlessness, insight, efficiency, and leadership skills. An industrial baron, an innovator, and a visionary, he was Henry Ford without the union trouble. His fatal flaw was weakness for his children. Sonny and Fredo could have done a little better with a few more whaps on their bottoms and a few less stolen carpets underneath them.

2. **Michael Corleone:** A worthy successor to the king, he had most of Vito's skills but was cursed with some unique fatal flaws—anger, hubris, and possessiveness. Even so, Michael might have actually owned the top slot in our rankings if not for his attitude in *Godfather, Part III*, where he spent the whole movie seeking absolution for his actions in GF1 and GF2. Come on, Mike. Don't spend two movies becoming one of the coolest characters in the history of cinema and then spend GF3 apologizing for it.

If he were a ballplayer, he'd be your Ted Williams/
Joe DiMaggio type—the gifted loner.

3. **Tom Hagen:** A Corleone in everything but name.
   Organized, intelligent, and loyal to a point. When
   you needed something extra-intimidating done,
   Tom was your man. He had the talent to run the
   entire shooting match, and might have if Michael
   hadn't gotten in the game midway through GF1. It
   was an amazing portrayal by Robert Duvall, who
   managed to make likeable a guy who cut off horses'
   heads and ordered prostitutes killed.

4. **Sonny Corleone:** Charismatic, brave, and brutal.
   Lacked emotional discipline and empathy to be a
   great Don, but was fun to watch. He would have
   made a hell of a Soprano, though. His temper got
   the best of him, and despite the multiple, obvious
   warning signs, he never took steps to control it;
   rather, he reveled in it. But when your enemies advise you to control your "famous temper," it's time to
   look into either anger management or Atavan. He
   looked good in a T-shirt and was a veritable ninja
   with a garbage can lid.

5. **Hyman Roth:** The top-ranked non-Corleone on our
   list. Roth was like one of those great old college foot-
   ball coaches, ala Joe Paterno or Bobby Bowden, who
   stay in the game just to spite people and show up the
   young guys. Hyman was so old, his first rap sheet was
   in Sumerian, yet he gave Michael all he could handle
   in GF2 and nearly brought down the franchise.

6. **Virgil "The Turk" Sollozzo:** The cause of all the
   trouble in GF1. Sollozzo brought narcotics to the
   Corleones only to have Vito turn up his nose at him

as if he had taken a line of cheap coke. Anticipating a "no," Sollozzo had a Plan B and unleashed a multi-pronged attack on the Corleones, "Pearl Harboring" them and nearly bringing them to their knees.

7. **Pete Clemenza:** Imagine Luca Brasi with an up-graded CPU and you have Clemenza. Clemenza is a guy you definitely want on your side. He was efficient with his hits and not bad with the sauce, either. I dated a girl once who thought his name was "Clem Enza" (as in, first name, "Clem"). I didn't fault her, though. For years, I thought Luca Brasi's name was spelled "Lou Cabrazzi."

8. **Fredo Corleone:** Most power rankings would have Fredo near the bottom, but being the dumbest member of the Corleone family is a lot like being the poorest member of the Hilton dynasty. In other words, it's still pretty good. Fredo had enough of a read on the situation to realize that Michael had marginalized him and to align himself with the best possible ally (Roth). Fredo was rightfully tagged early on as weak, and that's a hard label to shake. Loud tuxedos and Bud Abbott moustaches only added fuel to Fredo's image problems.

9. **Frankie Pentangeli:** An old-school Mafia opera-tive, fearless, outspoken, and shrewd, he was The Red Auerbach of the Corleone family. A fantastic performance by veteran character actor **Michael V. Gazzo** as "Frankie Five-Angels" earned him a Best Supporting Actor nomination that was ultimately won by Robert DeNiro. Though he was a pawn in the chess game between Michael and Hyman, Frankie never lost his cool or sense of humor.

10. **Don Fanucci:** A blustery buffoon, but those are the most dangerous kinds of buffoons. Fanucci was scary in a silent film villain sort of way, yet Vito spotted his intrinsic weakness and saw through the growling veneer. I was always intrigued by his country squire manner of dress—the garish white suit worn unabashedly amidst the squalor of turn-of-the-century New York City. Was he a walking ghost? Was he the man nobody could "touch"? His old-school pimp style was in direct contrast to the understated, earth-toned, Eddie Bauer style of Vito.

11. **Senator Pat Geary:** Had the balls to extort Michael Corleone while pointing his own toy cannon at him, and yet still ended up vacationing with him in Havana. Only a U.S. senator can be that duplicitous. His speech at the Corleone hearings, where he pumped up Italian Americans, was as priceless as it was pointless. Was he defending Michael and Italian Americans as a whole, or was he saying not to let a few rotten apples like Michael cloud our opinions of Italian Americans? To the best of my recollection, Geary represented the first time a U.S. senator was portrayed as so blatantly venal, diabolical, and, to use his own term, "oily."

12. **Connie Corleone:** The Eva Braun of the Corleones. She had a taste for blood, vengeance, and honor, but really poor taste in men. She gets this high by virtue of being the longest lived of Vito's kids, and if there were a *Godfather, Part IV*, I bet she'd still be hanging around, whispering murderous thoughts into the ear of whoever was running the show.

13. **Captain McCluskey:** I loved the sight of him in his bowtie and bowler, all dressed up for a relaxing night at Louie's Restaurant in the Bronx. Was it me or was his apologetic frisking of Michael on the fateful car ride to Louie's a little on the homoerotic side? McCluskey represented the worst side of New York's Finest and when he hit Michael with that John Wayne-like *Quiet Man* right cross, I swear I could feel it in my jaw.

14. **Luca Brasi:** Imagine Lenny from *Of Mice and Men* as a trained killer, and you've got Luca. Half-man, half-beast, he was the Sicilian Kung Fu Panda. When I first saw the "Luca Brasi sleeps with the fishes" scene, I could feel the chill and sense of unease in the room as Michael, Tom, and Sonny realized that they were in real trouble without their Frankenstein.

One of Luca Brasi's gangster AKAs was "Luca Eyeballs," small wonder (Lenny Montana from *The Godfather, Part I*, Paramount Pictures, 1974).

15. **Lou Woltz:** Foul-mouthed, dirty-dealing, exploitive movie mogul who brought new meaning to the phrase, "No business like show business." For a guy who probably produced light-loafered, post-war Technicolor musicals starring guys like Van Johnson and Dan Daily, Woltz was surprisingly at home dining with gangsters in his home. The implication: It's a lot tougher to make it in Hollywood than we think. I would have killed to be a fly on the wall in his office during a typical work day: "You tell that goddamned Fred Astaire to get the hell outta here, ya hear? I don't care how many tap dancing, ballet-influenced, soft-shoed creeps come crawlin' outta the woodwork!"

16. **Carlo:** Connie's husband. The Corleones had more than their fair share of trouble with Frankie Avalon-esque characters. After his experience with traitorous youngsters like Fabrizzio, Paulie, and Carlo, it's no wonder Michael spent most of GF2 in the company of his nameless Boris Karloff-type bodyguard.

17. **Tessio:** Looked like he had some potential as a young man, but slowly disintegrated into Abe Vigoda. Though he was supposedly the "smart one" of the Tessio/Clemenza pairing, I don't remember Tessio saying one smart thing in two movies. If he was "the smart one," then imagine how truly dumb they must have thought Clemenza was.

18. **Vincent Mancini:** Sonny's illegitimate son. A GF3 operative finally cracks the Top 25. Andy Garcia's operatic portrayal made Mancini seem more like a Godfather "fan" than a living, breathing character,

but he did bite off Joey Zaza's ear, predating Mike Tyson by more than two decades.

19. **Michael's Bodyguard in GF2:** Michael preferred having this Italian version of GORT for a bodyguard over a chatty, chummy companion, especially after his sour experience with Fabrizzio in Sicily, which ended in Fabrizzio murdering his first wife, the yummy and innocent Apollonia.

20. **Don Altobello:** GF3. When a Mafia Don exclaims, "What bread!" before eating some bread, you know he might be getting a little doughy upstairs himself. Altobello, played with jittery aplomb by the legendary Eli Wallach, provided more comical moments than menacing ones, especially his game of "Cannoli Russian Roulette" against Connie at the opera house. You bite-a. No, you bite-a!

21. **Michael's Bodyguards in GF1:** When Michael meets Apollonia, one of them says, "Careful. In Sicily, women are more dangerous than guns." I never understood the statement, but I guess it does explain why Italy did so poorly in both world wars. They underestimated how dangerous guns were.

22. **Mary Corleone:** An innocent who liked bad boys. Played by the lovely Sophia Coppola, who grew into a fine director in her own right. Sophia may have been an inexperienced actor, and reviews at the time zeroed in on her performance as one of the film's weak points, but I think her lack of acting "chops" gave Mary a sweetness that worked for that character. Originally, Winona Ryder was cast as Mary, but dropped out or was fired at the eleventh hour. I

think history will be kinder to Sophia's performance than contemporary critics were. Just as history will be kinder to Wynona Ryder as Mrs. Spock.

23. **Johnny Fontaine:** Al Martino was a good choice for the Sinatra analog, Johnny Fontaine, and was never really more than a footnote to the story. But when he comes back in GF3, a gray-haired and tinted-glasses-wearing eminence, it's more about nostalgia and reminding us that this was a Godfather movie than about anything else.

24. **Joey Zaza:** He was more "Gomer" than "Gotti," but I'll admit I can't take my eyes off of him when he's on screen. There was something childish and comical about Zaza. With Michael having to deal with guys like Zaza on a day-to-day basis, you can see why he was pushing so hard to go legit.

25. **B.J. Harrison (George Hamilton):** This was supposed to be the Tom Hagen role, but after Duvall dropped out because of a salary dispute, the character of B.J. Harrison was created. *The Godfather, Part III* had some intriguing casting choices (Eli Wallach, Andy Garcia, Joe Mantegna) and some loopy ones (Bridget Fonda, Hamilton, and Don Novello, formerly SNL's Father Guido Sarducci), but the loss of Duvall crippled the picture right out of the gate. When Wynona Ryder dropped out, the project began to take on the air of *Apocalypse Now, Again* a notoriously chaotic production.

The Official CORLEONE Aptitude Test

Still not sure who you are? You're about to find out. This test was designed to identify which of the core Corleones (Vito, Michael, Sonny, Tom, or Fredo) you tend to think and behave like. Armed with that knowledge, you can learn more about your strengths and flaws.

These questions have been designed to uncover your true Corleone. Don't try to figure out which answer is the "correct" one, because you won't be able to. Just check the first answer that comes into your head. Good luck!

1. Describe your role in your organization.
   a. I started the business and I run the show.
   b. I run a business that I inherited from an imposing, beloved, patriarchal figure. I never wanted to be in the business, yet, here I am.
   c. I'm training to be the new boss. Training stinks. I'm ready to rock and roll.
   d. I'm a trusted, behind-the-scenes guy. I like my role.
   e. I get sent to do this. I get sent to do that!

2. What are your greatest strengths or talents?
   a. If I had to say, I would say hard work, determination, inner calm, and love of family.
   b. I'm a determined, calm, but ruthless leader. I might be a genius.
   c. I'm a dynamic leader. Cross me and you better watch it.

d. I'm intelligent and committed, and keep business and personal separate.

e. I'm smart. Not dumb, like everyone says. I'm smart!

3. What are your weaknesses?

a. Deep in my heart, I'm a compassionate man. Maybe too soft on my kids.

b. I don't have any weaknesses. I try to bend people and events to my will.

c. I tend to be undisciplined and bad-tempered.

d. Sometimes I feel excluded from the true inner circle.

e. Some people say I'm stupid and weak.

4. Describe your marital status or family situation.

a. For me, there is only my wife and children.

b. Married to first wife. I'm happy, but I think she is secretly miserable.

c. Married, but I'm a lion. A lion needs more than one lioness. You know what I mean?

d. Married with kids. Sometimes I get lonely.

e. Married. My wife thinks I'm not a "real man." Whatever THAT means.

5. A business acquaintance does you an unexpected favor. How do you typically react?

a. I'm grateful. I know how to repay a favor.

b. I'm suspicious of unexpected gifts.

c. I kiss whoever it is, say, "C'mere," and maybe put them in an affectionate headlock.

       d. I gratefully accept in the name of my boss, and kick it up to him.

       e. No one's ever given me nothing, I think.

6. A trusted old employee comes to you and says he's unhappy.

       a. I listen to his grievances and make him feel important.

       b. I listen, but if it interferes with my plans, I blow him off.

       c. If I'm busy, I say, "Eh. Not now, huh?" If I'm not busy, I say, "Shaddup and do your job, huh?"

       d. I will listen, but I make it clear to him that I support my boss.

       e. I offer him a drink and show him a good time. That's what I do.

7. You have declined a partnership offer with a potential rival. You are concerned about his next move.

       a. I gather information by sending a spy in.

       b. I set plans in motion to kill the rival.

       c. I don't negotiate. I put a gun to someone's head and POW! I blow their brains all over their nice suit.

       d. I weigh options and negotiate on my boss' behalf, usually from a position of strength.

       e. I dunno. I get him a drink. Show him a good time?

8. How do you think others see your intelligence level?

       a. They respect me as seasoned old pro, but young Turks think I might be slowing down.

b. I think most people admire my intelligence and would like to have it.
c. I got your "intelligence" right here.
d. People see me as intelligent, tough, but reasonable.
e. People think I'm, like, dumb. But I'm not dumb. I'm smart.

9. How would you describe your drug and alcohol use?
a. I never touch it, except on special occasions. Unless I'm old and dying. Then I'll enjoy wine.
b. I drink or take these special pills daily. In my position, I need something to take the edge off.
c. Women are my drugs and alcohol. And, also, booze is, too.
d. Rarely. Only in times of extreme stress, like when telling my boss that his son is dead.
e. I'm what you call efficient. I use 'em both at the same time. Heh.

10. There is a juicy rumor going around about one of your co-workers.
a. I tell people I am not interested in things that don't concern me.
b. Information is power. You will always listen.
c. A little gossip can be fun. Especially about broads.
d. I'll listen, but you won't catch me doing it.
e. I'll listen and make an "OH MY GOD!" face. And maybe giggle.

11. You're nine years old and just witnessed your family being murdered by a local chieftain. You:
    a. Focus on survival. Revenge can wait.
    b. Wait until there is a large public ceremony like a wedding or baptism. Then you take care of all your enemies.
    c. Take your revenge. No talk about patching things up.
    d. Get vengeance, if there is a business advantage to it.
    e. Wait a second! I'm NINE years old?

12. You walk into a meeting intent on buying a business that the owner has no plans to sell. You:
    a. Tell him it's in his best interest, and that you would appreciate and repay this favor.
    b. Tell him he's doing a lousy job and to name a price.
    c. Hit him on the head with a garbage can lid and tell him to get out.
    d. Explain to him that your bosses are very motivated to get the deal done, and they never ask twice.
    e. Bang cocktail waitresses two at a time.

13. You confide in your best assistant that you have been keeping secrets from him for his protection. To ease his mind, you tell him:
    a. This is how it has to be. You give his cheek a loving pat.

b. That he's your brother and will be put in charge until matters are resolved.

c. You put him in a headlock and say, "What's the matter with you?" The message being that you love him.

d. In this example, you are the assistant.

e. None of this makes any sense to you. But you're smart.

14. You feel as if you are constantly passed over. Your move is:

a. Nothing. I'm in charge.

b. I'm in charge as well, but I watch out for people who think they are under-appreciated.

c. I'm next in line. I won't be passed over, unless I'm killed. Yeah, like that'll happen.

d. I understand my place, but it's frustrating. I could do a lot for this business.

e. I'm going to make a deal with a rival where there is something in it for me. For me!

15. A rival has unleashed a vicious verbal attack on you and your boss.

a. I never take it personally. But I strike back hard when it's advantageous.

b. I will take steps to eliminate all my enemies, even if it ultimately leaves me a shell of my former self.

c. No peace talks. No deals. Someone is going down.

      d. Sometimes you have to take defeats and attacks and move on.

      e. I forget what I should do in moments of crisis. I might cry afterwards.

Time to add up your score and see what category you fit into.

1) If you answered a) to at least nine of the questions, you are most likely a "**Vito**." Congratulations. You are likely on your way to the top, or you are already there. You don't need much help from this book, but it must be fun reading great things about yourself. You might benefit from review like an all-star ballplayer who revisits the "fundamentals" occasionally.

2) If you answered b) to at least nine questions, you are a "**Michael**." Again, congratulations are in order. You have what it takes to get to the top and stay there. But you have some serious flaws that could bring you down or stop your climb to the top. You'll need to get a handle on them or you could make more enemies than you can handle.

3) Frequent responders to question c) fall into the "Sonny" category. You are dynamic, if disorganized. You are independent and hands-on. Your communication style is direct and frank. You're the kind of guy who can get the ladies but never remembers their names. You will go places fast, but you don't have what it takes to stay there.

4) The Tom Hagens answer d) eight or more times. You are competent, intelligent, thoughtful, and valuable to your leaders. You are a natural consultant, and are most comfortable in

advisory or analytical rolls. You have the capacity to run the whole show and, in some ways, your value makes you a threat to your bosses. You have to walk a fine line to survive.

5) The Fredos answer e) eight or more times. First off, don't despair. Check our power rankings and you'll see that Fredo is not a lost cause, although your stupidity and weakness are constant hurdles to be overcome. We may not be able to make you less stupid, but I might be able to teach you some tricks to mask your stupidity and weakness.

* * *

In the subsequent chapters, we'll take a look at each of the core Corleones, starting with Fredo and working our way up to Michael. We'll learn how to redeem the Fredos and placate the Sonnies. In "Michael V. 2," we'll tweak the Michael in you to ensure the happy ending he never got and we'll advise the advisor with a chapter that talks directly, and calmly, to all of you Tom Hagens out there.

* * *

8. When Life Gives You Fredo, Make Fredo-Ade

FINDING OUT THAT YOU HAVE FREDO TENDENCIES CAN NEVER BE EASY. You can liken your Fredo revelation to a prostate exam: The test hurts, but not knowing what you have can hurt worse.

Regardless of how you did on the test, if you're constantly passed over for promotion or, worse, on the top of layoff lists, then you might be a Fredo. Your Fredo-ness is why your managers and colleagues shun you. Having Fredo tendencies means it's likely that the work you start never seems to get finished—and the few things you finish never seem to have any impact.

We all go Fredo once in a while. Sometimes, it's just an indicator that you need a vacation or an anti-depressant. Sometimes, your Fredo phase can go on indefinitely. You need to know how to fight your inner Fredo, or at least disguise him more effectively.

Growing up in the Bronx in the 1970s, we would play *The Godfather* instead of cops and robbers. No one wanted to be Fredo. Eventually, we came up with a rotating system with each kid taking his turn—a "designated Fredo."

Poor Fredo. Not even a twelve-year-old would play him. He's a profoundly uninspiring, despicable character. If he were a Spartan kid, Fredo would have been hurled off a cliff by his mortified parents. Fredo is stupid, yet not in a sympathetic way, ala

Lenny from *Of Mice And Men.* Fredo is reality-show-contestant stupid. He's an unredeemable, unrepentant idiot.

You're not really a Fredo, but you've probably sensed that something is missing. On the other hand, you may in fact be truly stupid and weak. But Fredo-level stupidity is, thankfully, rare. Nonetheless, you seem to share his tendencies and his outcomes.

Along with all his other faults, Fredo was a bad kisser (John Cazale, back to camera, and Al Pacino in *The Godfather, Part II*, 1974).

Blame—The Drug of Choice for Most Fredos

If you're a Fredo, you're likely blaming someone for your lack of success. Maybe it's your boss who "hates" you, or a colleague that undermines you, or a spouse that holds you back to fulfill his or her own ambitions. You may be right about your boss or partners and spouses, but how we deal with human obstacles marks the contrast between a Fredo and a Vito. **A Fredo blames them and lies down. A Vito eliminates them and moves on.**

Blaming people, even yourself sometimes, has become your drug of choice; we'll call it "Fredocontin." It makes you feel good in the short term, but damages you in the long term, and you are probably addicted to it. But this is your moment of clarity. As of this moment, you must stop blaming people, cold turkey. It's time to put down the Fredocontin for good and talk to the man in the mirror—the weasely, sweaty man in the mirror. If you don't, eventually, like other drugs, Fredocontin will kill you (although Michael helped a little). It will kill you emotionally when you run out of excuses and just start to sound crazy to most people. It will lead to failure after failure and, eventually, loneliness, a moustache, and a plaid tuxedo.

Blame is a derivative of self-delusion. You think you are somehow better than how most people see you, or, at the very least, misunderstood. You're in denial about your shortcomings. Your shortcomings are apparent to your rivals, who find it easy and fun to manipulate you and use you. You might as well be wearing the plaid tuxedo and pencil-thin moustache.

Fredo Triage—Stopping the Bleeding

As we said, it's a lot easier to *mask* being Fredo than it is to *stop* being Fredo. You have some hard-wired failure mechanisms. In the short term, you need to build up your self-esteem and change the way the world sees you. Fredocontin, or blame, won't do it. In fact, accepting the faults within you will actually make you feel better. You need some immediate stopgaps or triage to staunch your bleeding and keep you from falling further behind.

1. **Stop measuring yourself against other people**. You should only be in competition with yourself. Watching another person's success fuels your self-pity.

2. **When you compare your progress, change your metrics**. Don't measure the number of promotions or salary jumps. You'll only be discouraged. Measure instead, how much you've learned or improved over a given time period—how many things you did well in a day or a week versus how many you botched. Money and recognition come with accomplishment, not with pouting and blame. This is obvious to most people but, again, you're Fredo so it might not be as obvious to you.

3. **Accept responsibility for mistakes but NEVER apologize for them.** In a relationship, apologizing when you're wrong can make you a hero and get you make-up sex. In business, apologizing when you're wrong will get you screwed, but not the way you want. Apologies give your rivals an opening to blame you for problems. An apology can also create the perception that a mistake was worse than it really was. If you pay close attention, you'll see that only the most confident and secure people in an organization will apologize and accept blame. So never apologize. Say instead, "If I could do it again, I *might* do it differently." Try to pronounce the italics in *might*.

4. **Be gracious even if you have to pretend.** Nobody likes a sore loser. And nobody likes Fredo. So don't compound your sins. Be happy at someone else's good fortune. If you can't be happy, pretend. Karma is something you need on your side. Your immediate goals are damage control and stopping the air from leaking out of your career. Ambition and promotion should be something you should have on the back burner.

5. **Perform calculated acts of kindness.** Do the dishes for the wife without being asked. Play catch with the kid. Brush the dog. Or brush the kid and play catch with the dog. Create some goodwill for yourself with some calculated acts of kindness. Sure, it's calculated, but kindness is kindness. You win, and the thing you brush wins.

You won't go from Fredo to Vito in sixty seconds, but you will at least get out of the starting gate. With your ambitions, bitterness, and overt stupidity in check, you'll find less need to blame people. You might find yourself weaning off of the Fredocontin.

Fredometrics—The Fredo-to-Vito Ratio

In business, achievement needs to be tied to some kind of metric. A mortgage company might measure their delinquency rate to monitor loan origination quality. A hotel might look at the length of check-in, check-out times to measure service levels. A mob bookie might look at his profit to evaluate his line fixing skills.

Business improvements are driven by metrics. And since this is a book on business improvement, we're going to introduce our first metric: **the Fredo-to-Vito ratio.**

If you're in a Fredo funk, your F:V ratio is skewed toward your Fredo side. Fredo and Vito "events" drive the ratio. A Vito event is any event in which you react to stimuli and could honestly see Vito making the same decision or reacting the same way. The Fredo event is any event in which you react to stimuli and could honestly see Fredo reacting or deciding in the same manner.

Or in, other words, like *you* usually do.

To use your F:V ratio as a tool for continuous improvement, you can follow this simple method.

1. **Data collection**—For this step, any spreadsheet or journal will do. Data collection should only take a week before you can establish a benchmark. It's important that you log the following in your spreadsheet (you'll see why in the subsequent steps):

   a. Time

   b. Type of event—establish five to ten firm categories of work events. Examples include **meetings, lunches, presentations, socializing, business travel.**

   c. Briefly describe the event—"Boss asked me to stay late," "Boss threatened to take project away from me," "Someone keeps logging into my workstation," "I think everyone is snickering behind my back."

   d. Add a column called "**Emotions.**" Note a P for positive emotions and N for negative. You have to be honest here. Your descriptions of the events will help you to classify them. There are no right or wrong answers. Just feelings.

e. Add a column for **Outcome**. An outcome is the impact of your actions and feelings on this event.

f. Add a final column labeled "Corleone," where you note "Fredo" or "Vito" for your outcomes. Did you feel like "Fredo" made this decision or "Vito"? Your data should look something like this (see below)

Time:	9:30am
Event:	Meeting
Description:	Stupid Carl calls me in his office and says he's concerned with how I'm getting along with everyone. God. What an idiot.
Emotions:	Negative
Outcome:	I tell Carl everyone is out to get me, including him
Fredo or Vito:	Fredo

Time:	11:30am
Event:	Lunch
Description	Met Carl's boss. Now here's a guy I can talk to. I tell him Carl spends too much time worrying about team morale and chemistry and not enough

	about deadlines. He seemed to agree
Emotions:	Positive
Outcome:	He agrees to look into it.
Fredo or Vito:	Vito

Time:	2:30pm
Event:	Meeting
Description:	Presented stupid, waste-of-time GAP analysis. Typical of every meeting, stupid fat Danesh has to interrupt me every 10 minutes with "Why did you do it *this* way?" Because I'm not stupid like you, that's why!
Emotions:	Negative
Outcome:	People end up feeling sorry for the stupid slug, now I have everyone asking "Why did you do it this way?" Carl is looking at me like it's my fault and I can't get along with everyone. Can you imagine?
Fredo or Vito:	Fredo

2. **Analysis—**
   a. Add up your score. If you had fifteen "Fredos" and three "Vitos," your **F:V ratio is 5:1.**
   b. Look at the list for any trends. Do you make more Vito decisions in the afternoon or evening? Maybe your Fredo moments are a product of blood sugar crashes. Which events trigger your

Fredo response or negative emotions? Meetings? Presentations? Socializing? Identifying a trend or common factor in your Fredo incidents can help you mitigate their negative impact on you.

3. **Countermeasures**—This is where you make changes. This takes introspection—something that, as a Fredo, you might not have. You can find some effective countermeasures in the previous chapters. For example, if you're consistently nervous in meetings or thin-skinned when challenged, go back to the chapters on "Communication" or "It's Not Personal—It's Strictly Business." If you've done your data collection honestly (which is no, considering your state), you have the information you need to choose a countermeasure. Meaning, you should be able to identify your emotion and find a chapter that addresses it. Perhaps there might be something of value in other books.

4. **Data collect again and re-score**—How did you do on your second round? After a week of thinking about it, does Denesh still seem as stupid? Or smelly? Probably not. As you analyze and empathize, you realize that Denesh is not really a threat.

This is simple process-improvement methodology. Consultants get paid hundreds of thousands of dollars to implement projects based on these concepts. I just gave it to you for nothing. How very Fredo of me.

FredoRhythms—The Holistic Approach to Dealing with Your Inner Fredo

One could devote an entire book to the emerging science of FredoRhythms, the natural and holistic way to monitor your Fredo tendencies and channel the energy elsewhere. Let's just touch on a few simple rituals to cleanse or suppress Fredo tendencies.

- Morning rituals—A normal bio-rhythmic ritual would start with cleansing, meditative breaths. Since we're Fredo, let's just focus on our morning cigarette, making it a meaningful and relaxing ritual. Practice not being rushed. Feel that warm Marlboro Light smoke hit the back of your lungs. Fredo was always in a hurry and seldom relaxed, except when fishing. Ironically, this was a time when being nervous and edgy would have been appropriate, even life-saving.

- Turn your morning commute into a JOURNEY instead of a commute. Fredo likely had a tough time with commuting. You can picture him barking at pedestrians, his head out the window. Let's remove the tension. Close the windows. Turn off AM radio. Take an intellectual journey via a book on tape. Maybe this book is in your player right now? Talk about harmonic convergence. What if you are listening to this exact part of the book? Can you see now that the universe has a higher plan for you, Fredo?

- Respect all living creatures, including your co-workers. It may seem difficult, given the lack of respect they might have for you. Remember your Marlboro Light this morning. You were in control then. You're in control now. Think and show interest in your surroundings. Your surroundings will soon show interest in you.

You can see from this quick overview that mastery of your FredoRhythms can be a powerful tool. As mentioned, a serious look at FredoRhythms could fill an entire book, and this book is geared toward application of Godfather lessons in the workplace.

Low Hanging Fredo Fruit—Hitch Your Wagon to the Right Star

Here's another easy take-away to get you through your funk. As a Fredo, you're not really capable now of leading, innovating, or negotiating. You're limited now, so it's important that you hitch your wagon to the right star. Find the right ally or mentor and stick to him. Make yourself useful to him. Learn from him. The original Fredo did this fairly effectively in *Godfather, Part II*, aligning himself with Hyman Roth and Johnny Ola.

How do you tell who the right star is? Simple. He's the person who you most resent for their success. Aligning yourself with him/her will accomplish two things. First, you'll learn from proximity to someone with a clue, and second, you may come to learn that your resentment is unjustified.

Low Hanging Fruit, Part II

Sometimes all it takes is a list. I'm a big fan of lists. If lists will help you do a better job shopping, why won't they help you do a better job scheming or plotting? Here's a hypothetical list that Fredo could have used when he was deciding whether to betray his brother or not.

Should I Betray Mikey or Stick With 'Em?

Mikey

Is powerful
Backed up by plenty of muscle
Has ever-expanding interests
Sends me to fix nightclubs and stuff

Old Man Roth

Is powerful
Backed up by plenty of muscle
Has ever-expanding interests
Says there will be something in it for me

Next, it's important to identify emotional or personal reasons versus pragmatic reasons. A revised "Fredo Betrayal Decision List" would then look like this:

Mikey

Powerful
Backed up by plenty of muscle

Has ever-expanding interests
p- Sends me to fix nightclubs and stuff

Old Man Roth

Powerful
Backed up by plenty of muscle
Has ever-expanding interests
p- There will be something in it for me. For me!

The "p" signifies that this is a personal, not business-based, reason. **Personal reasons are useless and dangerous. Identify them and eliminate them from the list.**

Mikey	Old Man Roth
Powerful	Powerful
Backed up by plenty of muscle	Backed up by plenty of muscle
Has ever-expanding interests	Has ever-expanding interests

Now, both sides of the list are equal. Fredo's choice at this point would have been obvious: stick with Michael. Better the devil you know than the one you don't.

So, That's It? I'm Fixed?

All you need to do is recognize your own shortcomings, stop resenting people who are more talented or work harder than you, and work a little harder yourself. You're likely saying, "I can do that. Is that all?"

Well. No. If your funk has gone on for six months or longer, you probably need some psychological counseling, or a long heart-to-heart talk with one or both of your parents to help you consistently stick to a plan and silence the voices in your head. We can staunch the bleeding. You still have miles to go. Better get to it before you do something foolish. Good luck, Fredo.

Come back to us in four to six weeks and we will start again.

* * *

9. Your Sonny Disposition

WHEN SOLLOZZO THE TURK HIT VITO IN *GODFATHER, PART I*, HE CALLED SONNY TO NEGOTIATE AND SUGGESTED HE NOT "LOSE THAT FAMOUS TEMPER" OF HIS. *When your temper is so bad that even your enemies feel safe mocking you about it, you've got a bad temper.*

The most appealing thing about Sonny was also the thing that made him most vulnerable. He was uncomplicated. If things went bad, he was going to hit someone with a garbage can lid. If things went well, he was probably going to put someone in a headlock and give them noogies. That was Sonny. Scary or lovable, yet predictable.

Your responses to the scientific study show that you have some strong Sonny tendencies. Sonny is a seriously fatally flawed character, doomed from the outset, but not before he makes us fall in love with him. His literary equivalent is *Romeo and Juliet*'s Mercutio—quick-witted, combative, charismatic, and valiant. If you're not familiar with the classics, than think Riff from *West Side Story*, which was based on *Romeo and Juliet*. Not familiar with *West Side Story*? OK. Let's move on.

Sonny had two fatal flaws: his temper and maybe a sense of self-entitlement. He was the crown prince, and, as such, was likely to work a little less hard. He was also promiscuous, dangerously so. It could be that his anger drove him to be so promiscuous—his rages were temporarily placated by pleasures of the flesh. Well, all that stuff is part of the downside. Before we get into that, we like to look at our characters' upsides.

This was Sonny's idea of anger management. Images like this gave pharmaceutical companies the idea for Atavan, as in, "Hey, Look. Angry people like to swallow things" (James Caan and Talia Shire in *The Godfather*, Paramount Picture, 1972).

Sonny Side Up

Sonny had that animal magnetism thing—T-shirt, broad shoulders, and colorful Italian cadence. In this respect, he was more Soprano than Corleone. Had he been running strip joints and real estate scams in New Jersey, Sonny could have expected a long and happy life (gunned down at fifty instead of thirty-three).

Animal magnetism, charisma, charm, and sex appeal can be powerful assets in business. In fact, it's the basis of most highly successful sales careers. Which is why most of them are washed up by fifty, but not before they make a fortune, divorce a couple of wives, alienate a teenage daughter or two, and run up a tab at tanning salons across the country.

More upside? When you're a Sonny, people naturally like you. You're indomitable, tireless, and a lot of fun at times. Although you're doomed, folks will cry for you when you're dead, and at your funeral they will laugh and tell stories about the time you were thrown out of the Hilton for trying to beat up a bellman, or the time in New York when you paid the cabbie three hundred bucks so you could let the hooker you were with drive for a while.

You've got magic. You've got moxie. You've got sex appeal. What you haven't got is staying power. You will inevitably make that one fatal mistake. You'll first try to beat the system, then try beating it up. You'll tell off the boss. You'll go nuts in a meeting. You'll overturn a copier or smash a phone in a self-righteous rage. You'll disappear from work in a three-day pout, trying to make a point to management about how valuable you are—you may make your point but you'll seal your fate. Corporate management is like an organism. One cell goes astray, the rest will try to attack and digest it. Eventually, they will eliminate it.

So if you're Sonny, you're going to need to work on your staying power. You're going to need to learn to shut your yap without losing that spark that makes you Sonny. That volatility and raw energy that makes you so watchable will also be your undoing. Because just as it's easy to love the Sonnys of the world, it's relatively easy to kill them. Volatile people make enemies. Enemies make you dead.

Your Sonny scores also indicate a sense of self-entitlement. A sense of entitlement can make a person intellectually lazy.

It can also cloud or kill their sense of empathy. When Sonny was the interim Don, he was dependent on Tom, Clemenza, and Tessio for his information. He wanted things done, problems fixed, and wanted it now. He was unwilling or unable to see the big picture.

Though Sonny's screen time was short, his legacy looms large and his death was the defining tragedy of the saga. Credit for our enduring fascination with Sonny's character goes to James Caan, whose dynamic performance got him nominated for Best Supporting Actor of 1972, along with Al Pacino and Robert Duvall. Caan was the favorite going into the ceremony, but with three *Godfather* actors in the same category, the vote was sufficiently split for Joel Gray from *Cabaret* to steal the award, playing a prancing, pasty-faced anti-Sonny.

Turning "Santino" into "Sanity": Controlling that Temper of Yours

First thing's first...controlling the temper. If you are a Sonny, you are what was known up until the 1990s as a "hot-head." These days, it's known as bi-polar disorder or manic depression, which sounds a lot scarier to your colleagues than "hothead."

Once upon a time, before political correctness, the work-place was filled with Sonnys. They'd scream at the tops of their lungs, throwing phones against the walls while filling ashtrays to overflow. The hotheads were considered "do-ers." Every team had one. Their antics were tolerated because they were willing to go to war for a business. They were the ones who would scream at vendors to get supplies in on time. They were the ones who would tee-off on technical support personnel until the systems were back up and running. Every team had a Sonny on it and whenever opposing Sonnys met in battle, it was a thing of barbaric beauty.

Right around 1994, after the first sexual harassment suits, corporations got the idea that all sorts of harassing behaviors should be eliminated, including displays of rage. The idea of screaming bullies in the workplace became less and less tolerable to those who had to put up with them. Soon, every company was offering sensitivity training, communication training, racial/ diversity training and, of course, anger management.

Suddenly, Sonnys became scarcer. Many of them went underground, adapting to the new ways. But there are still a lot of latent Sonnys out there and you may be one of them. You have to manage that anger. Biting your fist does not count as "managing your anger." Nor does punching a wall, pulling your hair, or popping a Xanax.

There are some of you that take pride in your temper. You think others see your bombast as proof of your courage. Vito would see it as a sign of weakness. If you don't believe that managing your temper needs to be your top priority, then take a look at the table below. In head-to-head competitions, even-tempered players win more than their share of battles.

- **Patton vs. Eisenhower:** Easy going Eisenhower ended up Supreme Commander and benched the hot-headed Patton for the first quarter of Operation Overlord
- **Dr. McCoy vs. Mr. Spock:** McCoy was one helluva doctor, but his temper made him look silly and petty when going one-on-one against Spock

- **Russell Crowe vs. Jimmy Kimmel:** These two aren't in direct competition, but it's impossible to ignore the fact that the volatile Crowe's career continues to wane (he went from playing Maximus in *Gladiator* to chubby sociopaths in *Body of Lies* and *State of Play.* Meanwhile, with Letterman fading and Conan O'Brien and Jay Leno in flux, happy-go-lucky Kimmel is poised to become the new king of late night TV.

- **Ike Turner vs. Ringo Starr:** Ike's a Rock and Roll hall of famer, but most people remember him for giving Tina a fat lip. Lovable Ringo has spent nearly 50 years in the spotlight without so much as a misstep.

- **Donald Duck vs. Mickey Mouse:** Donald's hysterical rages have Daisy's friends wondering what she sees in the guy. Mickey on the other hand is "the logo".

- **Bugs Bunny vs. Daffy Duck:** I hate to go to the cartoon well again, but 5 seconds into their famous "Rabbit Season! Duck Season!" scene, you know who's going to come out on top. Bugs never got rattled, while Daffy had the second shortest fuse in the cartoon universe.

Take a good look. Now ask yourself which side you want to come down on.

Counseling/Analysis: Counseling is really the best, most sensible answer. Time to find out what makes you kick and scream. And if it's just "hot blood" (as it is for most Italian or Iranian men) then time to learn real techniques for controlling it. You may need to see a psychiatrist, someone who can prescribe anti-depressants. Anti-depressants can be dangerous, and, worse, cause impotence, so make sure you've exhausted your non-pharmaceutical options before going that route.

Visualization—Seeing Yourself Hitting Someone with a Trash Can Lid: This book is all about the quick fix. Try this quick-fix first, before you invest the time and tears in counseling. Psychologists often use "visualization" to help patients deal with anger, anxiety, or phobias. The classic example is fear of public speaking. To overcome it, you visualize your audience in a more vulnerable state than you; the classic example is visualizing the audience in their underwear.

As a Sonny, you would want to visualize your Sonny urges as a substitute for acting on them. So the next time your out-of-town boss treats you like expired dairy products while fawning all over your attractive lady assistant, visualize this: You drive up to the curb in your Packard. He recognizes you and smells the fire coming from your ears. He makes a run for it. You corner him and pound him on the head five or six times with a stainless steel trash can lid. For fun, toss in an image of the attractive assistant watching.

Visualization can be a key tool for dampening down self-destructive impulses. Give it a shot next time something goes against you.

Inner Calm = Visualization of You + Garbage Can Lid + Person who Messed with You.

Self-Entitlement: Crown Prince Syndrome

As first son, Sonny expected to inherit the family business and was, in fact, the crown prince until his death screwed with the line of succession. If you're in that kind of position, where you are working for your family business, or you have a friendly relationship with your boss (you call each other "big guy"), it's important not to give off airs of entitlement or expectation. It's also important that you work or at least *appear* to work as hard as the lower-born castes.

Any manager can fall into a "crown prince syndrome." They start to expect advancement. They gripe in front of employees. My favorite example of this was when my company was on the short end of a gigantic merger. We were all worried about a layoff, so my manager called us in for a little reassurance, town hall style.

"I just want you guys to know that I'm not going anywhere. But if things get weird, they can fire me, I don't care. I have a year's severance, and I make $250,000 a year, so f__ them."

Whew. I felt better.

Time and time again, spoiled managers have sown the seeds of resentment that turn into betrayal. Without knowing much about Carlo, it's possible he got a little fed up with Sonny's perpetual head locking and bossiness, not to mention poundings with garbage can lids.[2] If you are a crown prince, be careful about what you say and how you say it around your plebes. Try not to complain too loudly about your salary, or gripe about your father's good health and unwillingness to die

---

2 Little touches make a movie great. Sonny's pounding of Carlo was an inspired and possibly improvised moment of either acting or directing genius, courtesy of either Mr. Coppola, who may have said, "It's not working for me. Try hitting him with that garbage can lid," or Mr. Caan, who, in the midst of method acting fury, caught sight of that gleaming trash can lid and followed his emotional impulse. Together they created a moment that made some people turn away in sympathetic pain, some laugh in malevolent glee, and that nobody would ever forget.

or retire, thus leaving you in charge. You're better off *pretending* to be one of the guys, all the time knowing that you have better DNA. Put in some extra hours occasionally, instead of leaving early every day. Every once in a while, roll up your sleeves and show the troglodytes what you can do.

Try to be more like Prince Harry and less like Prince Charles and you'll be on track.

A Sonny Outlook

Sonny's anger and intellectual laziness made him dependent on Tom and Clemenza for ideas and answers. Fortunately, Mike stepped up in time to save the family as a whole, but not Sonny. Sonny's flaws made him a monolithic thinker, one who looks at events with one viewpoint.[3] He lacked "empathy."

If you manage to suppress your anger and embrace a little humility, you'll start to develop your empathic abilities. You do that, and pretty soon you start to question things a little more closely.

You have the makings of a leader but you keep shooting yourself in the foot and hitting others on the head with garbage cans. If you can work out your anger issues and learn to work a little harder, you're outlook is bright, even sunny, Sonny.

* * *

---

3 The term "monolithic thinking" sounds pretty cool, but was just made up by me. There's nothing there. Don't bother Wikipedia about it. They have enough baloney to fix.

10. Tom Hagen—Number Two with a Bullet

YOUR ANSWERS INDICATE THAT YOU ARE THAT TOM HAGEN-TYPE IN YOUR ORGANIZATION, OR AT LEAST YOU THINK YOU ARE. You've worked hard to get to the "near top." You're well paid, valued, and people know that when you speak, you speak for your manager. This makes you a tremendously valuable resource to your boss.

So why are you so uneasy? In short, you may be so good at your job that your boss doesn't trust you. He/she suspects that you may have your sights set on the top spot. He/she might think you're being recruited by the competition. He/she may be jealous of the attention you get.

Then again, you might in fact be looking for that top spot, but can't convince anyone that you can do the job, since they see you only as a second banana. You might be so good in your role that they can't afford to promote you.

This is a delicate spot to be in and certainly not one you deserve to be in, given all you've done for your company. You "Toms" out there have to do a delicate survival dance, and it seems unfair given all you've put into your job. You're aware of the resentment and the distrust, yet your typical past response, to work harder or be more loyal, only earns you more enmity.

The Strength of Hagen

My father used to refer to Tom as a "piece of bread," a literal translation of an old Venetian colloquialism. It was generally used for all-around good guys, or in English, a good egg. Tom, of course, was nothing of the sort. Tom was ruthless and tough, an orphan from the mean streets of Depression-era Manhattan who managed to cling to survival long enough to catch the attention of Vito, who adopted him.

Doesn't sound like a piece of bread to me. Vito must have seen the strength in this feral tiger. He subsequently caught him, raised him, and sent him to law school, giving the Corleones an edge that no other family had: a consigliere with a law degree who was probably *also* a notary public. So, while other gangs had guys named "Knuckles" and "Joe Salami" as consiglieres, the Corleones had in Tom a resource that was one part Terminator, one part Roy Cohn—relentless, determined, and indestructible.

The Problem with Being Hagen

The problem with the Tom Hagens of the world is not with their personalities; rather, it's with the way they are perceived. Number Twos can face some challenging circumstances.

- If they are Number Two too long, people wonder what's wrong with them.
- If they are better at the job than Number One, tensions can arise.
- If something falls through the cracks, you can become perceived as a bottleneck.

Always a Bridesmaid List: Numbers Twos Who Couldn't Break Through

There is a danger in being a Number Two for too long. Your reputation and prospects turn into "number two." Number Twos who never break through to become Number Ones tend to diminish in stature over time. Then oftentimes the perception becomes that their more talented, dynamic partners carried them.

1. **Al Gore:** Distanced himself from Bill Clinton in the latter years of their administration, then lost to George W. Bush, which set every 2012 prophecy into high gear. Now he's the punch line for every joke about global warming or the Internet.
2. **Art Garfunkel:** Paul Simon wrote all the songs, but Garfunkel treated his time in Simon and Garfunkel like it was detention. A little more public gratitude toward Simon would have served him well. And it might have earned him a guest shot on *The Muppets* too.
3. **Ed McMahon:** Sitting next to Johnny Carson made Ed seem funnier than he was. Everything in Ed's life seemed to go south after Johnny's retirement, including, well, his life.
4. **Scottie Pippen:** Tried to equate his impact as equal to Michael Jordan's, which is a lot like Jimmy Olsen saying he contributes as much as Superman. Spent 4 seasons in Houston or Portland, trying to get one more ring than Jordan.
5. **Hilary Clinton:** She lives in two shadows: Barack Obama's and Bill Clinton's. In the 2008 campaign,

she lost to the then unknown Obama, making her a rare double Number Two. Her outburst during an African diplomatic trip ("Go ask my husband what he thinks!") showed how deep her Number Two wounds are.

6. **Steve Ballmer:** Co-founder and current CEO of Microsoft. If there's any doubts that Bill Gates was the genius, check the price on Microsoft stock the past ten years.

7. **Donald Duck:** A distant Number Two to Mickey. When you're a cartoon character and the Disney Corp. still can't figure out what to do with you after seventy-five years, you're a lousy cartoon character. Even ducks have gotten fed up with waiting for his breakout performance.

8. **Dan Akroyd:** A singular talent, yet every year he was on *Saturday Night Live*, he was never better than the second-best cast member. Every movie in which he was a lead was a mess. He did OK whenever he co-starred with a headliner (Bill Murray in *Ghostbusters*, Eddie Murphy in *Trading Places*, John Belushi in *Blues Brothers*) only cementing his air of two-ness.

9. **John Adams:** American history's greatest Number Two was underappreciated in his time and apparently miserable over it. Less charismatic than Jefferson. Less ingenious than Franklin. Less inspiring than Washington. The ultimate irony was that he was elected our first VICE president (second in command) and our SECOND president. Thankfully though, his contributions have been appreciated

and his place in the Pantheon of American history is secure. The only member of the founding father's Big 4 (Franklin, Washington, Jefferson, Adams) without an impressive monument or museum to his name.

10. **Alan Colmes:** Of *Hannity and Colmes.* As the resident democrat on "Hannity," he did more damage to liberal causes than Jane Fonda, Alec Baldwin, and Al Sharpton all rolled into one, as he let Hannity beat his brains in every night.

Eventually, every Number Two should try to step out on his/her own and try to make it as the top dog. Just remember that the cost of failure is unfairly high. History calls you a "second banana" for the rest of your career.

Uneasy Lies The Head that Doesn't Want to Wear the Crown

In a perfect world, a grateful boss would want to recognize and reward the loyalty of a Tom Hagen. Unfortunately, that is not always the case, as you Tom Hagens of the world are finding out. There are a lot potential landmines in the relationship between a manager and his consigliere.

1. **Why Do I Need This Guy Syndrome**—Some Number Twos think their only job is to make the big guy look good. Don't make that mistake. The big guy actually starts to believe that he's the one who gets stuff done. If you work to get the big guy promoted, don't count on his taking you with him.

2. **Reverse Jealousy Syndrome**   This happens when
    people go to you instead of him. You are starting to
    get recognition outside of the fold and he/she doesn't
    like it. Technically, you should be jealous of her,
    given her pay grade, but it's reversed. Some signs
    of R.J.S. include:
    *   Your boss keeping his door closed more
    *   Inexplicable silent treatments
    *   Laughing overly loud on phone conversations so
        you overhear and maybe get jealous

Some Hagen-Style Countermoves

So you have this perverse situation where you've propped
up your boss only to have him/her turn on you. You sense your
boss may be making a move on you. You need to control your
turf and stick up for yourself. Hopefully, at this time, you've
learned enough to know that the boss isn't a friend or a mentor.
Just a guy one pay grade above you, so you won't take any of
what he does personally. There are subtle ways to let him know
that you are no fool and that you are no coward.

*   Put a very visible Post-It on your terminal with the
    words "Call HR."
*   Drop all friendly accents out of your emails to
    him—no more "hi" or "hey." If he wants to "go to
    the mattresses," so can you.
*   Print everything, then file it and lock it in your desk.
    Make sure that he sees you doing it occasionally.
*   Exaggerate your relationship with the big bosses.
    Ask him sometimes if he knows where the big boss

is. If he says, "I don't know," you immediately snap your fingers as if you remembered something and say, "Oh! That's right! That thing with his wife." If your boss says, "Why do you ask?" you can really make him nuts with, "I left my Bluetooth in his car."

The Bottleneck Syndrome (or "Key-Man Dependencies")

If you run the whole show for your department, you may feel tremendous satisfaction and genuinely enjoy the role, but eventually someone is going to point out to your boss that his dependency on you is a kind of risk. Ouch.

It's a tough place to be in. You've taken on every assignment, and when problems arise, you always clear your plate for more. You've designed the systems. You manipulated the data or analyzed it. You've blazed trails, yet it's gotten you into trouble. Outside auditors tend to zero in on you as a "bottleneck." That's usually because they need to submit some kind of "findings" to justify their billing rate. So even a department that runs like clockwork can get dinged when only one person (you) truly knows how that clock works.

The key here is to recognize that you're a "key-man" before they do and to have put it down on paper that you think the department would run better with more people involved. You don't have to actually believe it, but you should have gotten it in writing.

Auditors tend to be cute about potential findings, especially key-man findings, and they like to play good cop to get you to open up. So when the auditor says, "So you're able to do ALL this yourself? Great! I bet you must be tired. Ha, ha," you can say, "Yes, but I do have concerns that too much may be running through this desk. Can I show you my plans to address them?"

I know it would be much more palatable to say, "I have no time for your stupid questions. I have a whole department to run," but that would be making their point for them.

Counseling the Consigliere

Ultimately, you're going to have to make a choice: stay where you are and keep a close eye on the people above you, or make a move. If you find yourself worrying too much about hidden meanings, or what your boss might think about what you say, then it's probably time to look elsewhere.

As Thoreau once said, *"I would rather sit on a pumpkin and have it all to myself, than be crowded on a velvet cushion,"* which I choose to interpret as, "It's better to strike out on your own, even to fail on your own, than to serve forever at someone else's whims." So when the time is right, Tom, go out and start your own family, and you can really give your boss something to worry about.

* * *

11. A Wise and Considerate Young Man

MICHAEL CORLEONE IS, OF COURSE, THE CENTRAL FIGURE IN THE GODFATHER MOVIES HE WAS THE GOLDEN CHILD, THE CHOSEN ONE. Gifted and hard working, he grew the empire to new heights and found a strength he never thought he had as the new Don. If you're a Michael, as your test scores show, you're a visionary leader, the type who can take a million-dollar business and grow it into a billion-dollar one.

How is it that someone with all that money, all that power, and all that intelligence can still end up in the dumps? Michael ended up lonely and soulless, yet on the surface he appeared to make very few mistakes. Michael's biggest flaw may have been his arrogance. Sitting in his Nevada palace, in his ascot, with slicked back hair, and immersed in a fog of filter-less Camel smoke, the Michael of *The Godfather, Part II*, was an aristocratic fop version of the squeaky clean Michael of GF1. It could be that reason, coupled with his brutally dull personality, that may have provoked old guys like Hyman Roth, Senator Geary, and Frankie Pentangeli to mess with him, or get in his face occasionally. Even Fredo was fed up with Michael's act and took matters into his own fumbling hands.

So things spiraled out of control for Michael, and rather quickly. By the time we catch up to him in *The Godfather, Part III*, his gray hair cropped short and straight, Michael is a lost soul, spending his remaining years trying to make an uneasy peace with God and his family. What's worse, he's hanging out with Father Guido Sarducci (Don Novello) and George Hamilton. How did he fall so far?

As a Michael, you're no stranger to success. You need to stay humble and hungry, so that the people you passed on the way up don't start gunning for you.

Scarred Face: After his jaw was broken by Capt. McCluskey, Michael's ugly side came out.

Michael V. 2

If Michael had been a little more humble, would his life have turned out differently? He was a near billionaire by the time he crumbled to diabetic dust in *The Godfather, Part III*, yet he had little peace of mind. If he were a humble man, like Vito, his attacks would have come mostly from outside the organization. People stuck by Vito, yet liked to stick it to Mike.

It's likely that given a little more people skills, he could have dodged the following:

1. Fredo's betrayal
2. Connie's crazy Rat Pack phase
3. Hyman's assassination attempts
4. Frankie's temper tantrums
5. Tessio's sell-out
6. Don Altobello's whatever the hell that was in *The Godfather, Part III*
7. Joey Zaza's aerial attack in *The Godfather, Part III*

That's a lot of animus generated from being cocky, but that's the motivating power of arrogance. If you are a little punk at this point, recognize that there is a core insecurity driving it (fear of failure, lack of stature, etc.) and tackle that, instead of beating people over the head with your money and power.

Without these seven headaches, all probably driven by a need to show him up, Michael's life would have turned out very differently, and he (and we) might have been spared *The Godfather, Part III*.

What kind of Michael would we have had if he had dined regularly on Humble-Roni? George Bailey-style, we can look at what the world would have been like with a nicer Mike. How many lives would be forever changed?

1. Fredo—Fredo would have never felt the need to usurp Michael. He would have eventually been promoted to director of casino operations for all the Corleone properties. With the support of his family, he would have ditched his crazy wife for a

nice Italian girl (a widow that Connie met at a local PTA meeting), settled down, had kids, and died in 1979 in a jet skiing accident.

2. Connie—Connie's rebellious, drinking, Rat Pack-style globe-hopping and sleeping around phase would have been agreeably shorter. Always an independent lady with a head for business, Connie would have gotten her Realtor's license and made her own small fortune selling homes for the Reno and Tahoe Century 21 offices.

3. Hyman—without the aggravation of having to go head to head with Michael during the span of GF2, Hyman would have started to think seriously about retirement, and he eventually would have. Then he would have focused on his health, got better, and lived twenty more years, establishing the Hyman Roth wing of Northwestern Hospital in Chicago.

4. Frankie Pentangeli—Frankie would never have gone off on Michael, so he would have never suspected that Michael had it out for him. Frankie would eventually die in a choking accident on Christmas Eve, 1967.

5. Tessio—Tessio, the smart one, would have stayed put and died a solid Number Three in the Capo regime behind Clemenza and Barney Miller.

6. Don Altobello—Altobello would have never had to face Connie's cannoli cannonade. With Michael's move to legitimacy, he would have bought ten thousand shares of International Immobilare, and would have died peacefully in his bed in Sicily in 1981.

7. Joey Zaza—Zaza and Michael could have existed peacefully, with Joey being the media "King of New York" and Michael benefiting from the press' Zaza fixation. Eventually, Joe would get indicted for a scandal involving the bribery of an OTB official. Representing the prosecution in the Zaza case would be a brilliant, ambitious federal prosecutor named Rudy Guiliani, who managed to get a conviction for racketeering, putting Zaza on ice for years.

Arrogance-Masking Techniques

If you're a successful and arrogant S.O.B. like Michael, people are going to be gunning for you. There are several archetypes that are sensitive to arrogance, and you need to know them so you can throw them with some false humility.

1. **Old Guys**—Old guys love making life miserable for a younger, more successful rival, especially if he is arrogant. Michael had trouble with all sorts of old guys, including Hyman Roth, Frankie Pentangeli, Don Altobello, Tessio, Captain McCluskey, and Senator Pat Geary. The only old guy Michael didn't have any trouble with was Vito. **Arrogance-masking tips:** Try calling them "sir" a lot. Old guys eat that up.

2. **Siblings**—Sibling rivalry is really kind of a misnomer. It should be called "sibling resentment" because if both siblings were successful, then they'd tend not to be rivals. In Michael's case, he was saddled with two doozies in terms of resentment:

Fredo and Connie. **Arrogance-masking tips:** If you're successful and have a dumb ass for a sibling, hire one or both to be your "managers." Pay them a decent salary and give them harmless things to do like taking care of your car or paying your gardener.

3. **Genuinely Stupid People of All Ages (or GSPs)**—GSPs, as a rule, hate successful people. They don't seem to appreciate the work and sacrifice a successful person has to make during a career, and they attribute their success to luck, nepotism, or someone having pictures of someone. I've heard the "having pictures on someone" reason given innumerable times as an explanation for someone's promotion or staying power. In twenty years in corporate America, I've yet to see a single set of pictures on anyone. A smart and arrogant person would tend to avoid GSPs, only increasing their resentment. To their credit, GSPs can usually detect when a person is genuinely avoiding them. **Arrogance-masking tips:** Suck it up and have lunch occasionally with some GSPs. You will experience something close to the bending of the laws of physics as time comes to a near halt in what will undoubtedly be the longest hour of your life, but if you do it once in a blue moon, you can keep the GSPs at bay. Make sure you pay for the lunch and, for fun, make sure you take your car. The GSP will appreciate riding in style.

Michael Corleone, His Family and His Family

Michael comes into the world brimming with intelligence and courage. He is doted on by his family and flourishes in college and on the field of battle. In a time of crisis, he saves his father's life and business and eventually succeeds him, then supersedes him. He makes plans to expand and revolutionize his business, hoping to go legitimate with a snappy Five Year Plan (which he'll launch at the next company meeting). He appears to be a responsible patriarch and a loving father and husband.

Then it all goes south in a hurry. His brother Fredo turns on him, and Michael is in the fight of his life with a deadly rival. His wife, Kay, grows to despise and fear him, eventually leaving him. His closest allies begin to dread him. He grows more and more ruthless and, as *Godfather Part II* progresses, we see the humanity and spark draining out of his eyes.

The fall of Michael Corleone re-enforces some pretty obvious lessons about life, the most obvious being that doing evil, no matter how well intentioned, will destroy you and the ones you love.

In working hard to protect his family, Michael lost his *family*.

Very few of us will achieve Michael's level of success, and fewer of us still will have unleashed his measure of malfeasance onto the world, but we can still learn from his mistakes.

The lesson that evil in the name of service to your family is wrong seems to run counter to the over-arching lesson of the book: that you can do bad things at work, expect bad things from people, and still be a good person at home.

But Michael did not execute "It's Not Personal..." as well as Vito did. Michael changes over the course of *Godfather Parts I and II*. We see him drink more. He's popping pills. He smiles less and less and eventually, not at all. He's sullen, dull, and ghoulish.

Vito, on the other hand, burdened with a similar legacy of sin, somehow managed to keep things lighter and jauntier around the Corleone home. Granted, he wasn't a barrel of laughs either, but he was practically Merv Griffin compared to Michael. Vito started the business and chose his path, whereas Michael felt forced into it. So the sins may have weighed heavier on him.

All the MORE reason for Michael to try to keep it light and try to separate the business and the personal. Would it have killed him to dress like Santa around Christmas time or take his wife, kid, and a few bodyguards to Yosemite once a year? How about some water skiing on beautiful Lake Tahoe? How about maybe taking a few minutes out of his day to order Rocco or Al to play catch with his son?

Little touches like this go a long way. Michael forgot the basics. He forgot how to compartmentalize. This inability to keep business and personal separate became the premise of *Godfather III*. So what can we really learn from the fall of Michael Corleone?

That "It's Not Personal..." really works.

* * *

12. It's Called Organized Crime for a Reason—It's Organized

More Meet = Less "Meat"

IN TODAY'S WORKPLACE, IT'S EASIER THAN EVER TO HOLD A MEETING. Technology is making the world a smaller place, and that's unfortunate, because most of us hate meetings. Most of us dread meetings the way Edgar Allen Poe dreaded black cats and ravens. Technology may be bringing us together, but most of us want to wring technology's neck for it.

We meet more and accomplish less and less. We've made it too easy to meet. Send out a meeting notice, set up a WebEx session, and voila, a dozen or so people show up with nothing to say. Rather than think, we meet.

It's not that meetings per se are useless. Historically, meetings have provided human beings with some of their greatest moments. The Continental Congress was a meeting. Nixon *met* Mao Tse Tung and opened up relations with China. The post-WWII map wasn't decided on the battlefield. It was decided in meetings held in Tehran, Yalta, and Potsdam. The smell of coffee and Danish, not cordite and smoke, filled the air as the fate of Western civilization was discussed.

Meetings are essential tools for commerce. But like everything else in corporate culture, they have been diluted to the point of uselessness by the lack of direct communication and the pointless consideration of everyone's viewpoint.

We hate meetings because they are a waste of time.

Not all meetings are a waste of time. Nixon and Mao took care of business in 1972 and there wasn't a Danish or a PowerPoint in sight.

Your Typical Meeting vs. a Corleone Conference

Here's a rundown of a typical meeting in today's corporate culture. See if this pageant of pointlessness sounds familiar:

Eight o'clock is the scheduled starting time. Eight is significant because it's the cutoff hour for someone to bring Danish or bagels for a meeting. People trundle in, fidget, and nod at each other. The room is filled with people who aren't sure why they are there.

The organizer starts the meeting, but instead of getting right to the point, he or she sits and preambles with a long, dissembling greeting, rambling incoherently like a recovering addict in group therapy about what an important meeting this is and thanking everyone for coming. Meanwhile, her assistant passes out THE HANDOUTS with all the seriousness of launch codes. They bear the corporate logo and the warning "FOR INTERNAL DISTRIBUTION ONLY," as if anyone would be selling these on the street like scalped Rolling Stone tickets. These precious handouts will soon be internally distributed into the trash no longer than one minute after the meeting ends.

Sometimes there are remote participants, which means conference lines or webinars. Inevitably, there's trouble with the equipment and at the first sign of trouble, chubby guys spring from their chairs like first responders at a tenement fire and begin a mad dash in and out of the room looking for cables. No one knows why they always think it's "the cable," but invariably, they do. One of them will bark, "I used to work for IT!" as he dives heroically under the table, cables wrapped around him like bandelero.

Tense minutes pass as the meeting facilitator smiles woodenly, waiting for the dumpy ex-IT guy to extract himself from the table and for the show to go on. As his submergence continues for three, maybe five, minutes, tension levels rise. A second chubby ex-IT guy offers his assistance. Some of the higher-ranking attendees start to look at their watches, a significant gesture of impatience that is picked up on by the facilitator.

For a moment, you let yourself hope that the meeting may get post-poned due to the technical difficulties. But inevitably the facilitator, feeling the time pressure and sensing the walls crumbling down around his meeting, breaks down and growls, "Just forget about it! We'll move ahead without the visuals!"

The chubby guys slink back into their seats and the Voyage of the Damned continues.

Once the meeting begins in earnest, the facilitator is constantly inter-rupted with questions, or corrections. It seems like everyone wants to say *something. CO_2 levels start to rise. Sugar highs from the 8:00 a.m. Danish are wearing off and after forty-five minutes of meaningless gab, you start to shut down. You fight it off but the sense of mental fatigue is overwhelming and soon you're yawning like an infant in a car seat. Your oxygen-starved, under-stimulated brain has giving up. You want to lie down in a corner and just fall asleep like a frozen mountain climber succumbing to altitude sickness—the fatigue and sense of futility are THAT overwhelming.*

Another meeting. Another sixty minutes you'll never get back.

Does that all sound familiar? Contrast that torture to some of the meetings you've seen in *The Godfather*. In a Godfather meeting, the core issues get discussed. The dialogue is direct. The objectives are clear and understandable. Best of all, it only takes about five to ten minutes.

Your meetings stink by comparison, don't they? To be fair, you're not Francis Ford Coppola or Mario Puzo, so no meeting you facilitate will have the dramatic flair that these two masters can stuff into a scene. In fact, nothing you ever do will have that flair. But that doesn't mean you can't learn a thing or two from them in terms of keeping things brief.

By the same token, you're not Al Pacino or Robert Duvall, so you'll never be as compelling or dynamic as they can be. But that doesn't mean that you should be rambling on when you are speaking, or yawning like a three-month-old when you're not.

H.A.G.E.N.: A Five-Point Meeting Planner

Meetings provide some of the most memorable moments in *The Godfather* world, whereas your meetings are significant only in that they shorten life spans. The key distinction between Godfather meetings versus your meetings is their brevity. In

The Godfather, it's five to ten minutes, tops, and people are back in their cars, setting schemes in motion.

You probably think that a five-minute meeting is as doable as time warp or pre-11:00 a.m. check-in at a hotel, but it is doable, provided other guidelines that define the content and tone of a meeting are adhered to. Below are the rules of engagement as I see them for the typical Godfather-style meeting. Together they form a set of rules for holding meetings that I call "**H.A.G.E.N.**" in honor of the most well-organized, efficient member of the Corleone clan, Tom Hagen. Here are the main points of H.A.G.E.N.:

H - Have a FIRM objective for the meeting.
A - Always be direct.
G - Get the principals speaking.
E - Everyone else shuts up.
N - No meeting should last more than ten minutes.

We'll look at the rules and then apply them to the most famous Godfather meetings to see how the rules drove them. Meanwhile, start thinking about how nice it would be if your meetings were that simple and efficient. Like blocking out the emotional noise in chapter 1, imagine if you could eliminate the chubby ex-IT guy under the table forever.

H - Have a FIRM Objective for the Meeting

A firm objective keeps your meeting brisk and focused. It also becomes the benchmark for your meeting's success. If your objective was to "designate a project manager" then you can measure your success simply in terms of "Did you designate a project manager?"

Meetings are a place to work. There should always be a reason to meet, a task to accomplish, an assignment to give, and so on.

If you can't come up with a firm objective then the meeting doesn't need to be called. Believe it or not, a lot of people don't know the difference between a firm goal or objective and ephemera. Here's a pop quiz. Which one of these is a firm objective?

> Discipline Larry.
> Set Place and Date for Larry's Surprise Party.

If you said "Discipline Larry," then you are going to need to buy another copy of the book. The correct answer is "Set Place and Date for Larry's Surprise Party." While "Discipline Larry" sounds "firm" because it has discipline in it, it is complete fluff. It's fluff because it's impossible to say at what point is Larry disciplined. Disciplined, yes or no, is impossible to measure.

A - Always Be Direct (Good Communicators vs. Good Bullshitters)

Tom, Vito, and Mike were direct communicators. This, of course, is the function of the brilliance of Coppola and Puzo, expert storytellers who know how to write dialogue that resonates. As previously noted, you're not Coppola or Puzo. You'll never be able to consistently create dialogue that effective. But shouldn't you at least try, especially when there is a bunch of people in one room?

In corporate America, today, too many of us are circumspect, repetitive, long-winded, and dull (much like this sentence). If you can be direct and concise, you'll be miles ahead of the other guys in the meeting who are too busy "running it up flag poles" and "thinking outside of the box" to actually make a real point. Effective communication equals money and power, but it doesn't necessarily mean accuracy or honesty. In other words, how you say something is more important than what you actually say. You could be lying, distorting, finger-pointing, or just being plain wrong, but if you are DIRECT, you'll actually sell your point more effectively than the equivocators.

Effective communication doesn't necessarily mean imaginative or entertaining communication. In corporate America, there are a lot of characters that affectionately refer to themselves as "good bullshitters," but these guys are kidding themselves. The secret to good communication is a capacity for directness, not bullshit. For H.A.G.E.N. to work, you will have to be blunt, direct, and brief. The perfect example of this mode is Michael's classic offer to Senator Geary in GF2.

> "My offer is this. Nothing. Not even the fee for the gaming license, which I would appreciate if you put up personally."

There is a lot of poetry in that statement, especially as read by Pacino, with a mix of bemusement and menace. But this moment says more about Michael than any off the other bits of dialogue. What do we learn about Michael from this terse little declaration?

- Michael was offended by the Senator's reference to his "family"
- Michael of Godfather Part II was all business all the time and a heck of a lot scarier than Vito.
- Michael has to fight harder to overcome the perception that he's a kid, a punk or in over his head. So he shows his teeth more easily

It's a perfect little bit of movie making – loaded with subtext, yet that subtext is clear as a bell. See for yourself. Pop in the DVD. I dare you not to mutter "Whoa…"

Corporate Newspeak: "Houston, We Have an Opportunity"

We are constantly tweaking the language to make negative terms sound more palatable or positive. "Employees" have become "associates"; a "crisis" becomes a "challenge." This "corporate Newspeak" really started to take off in the mid-'90s with the concurrent ascendance of HR and IT in the workplace. Both these entities introduced volumes of fluff-a-nutter into the lexicon.

The more we rely on corporate Newspeak, the less effective we become. How many times have you been in a meeting where nobody would say what needed to be said? The boardrooms of America are being overrun with eight-hundred-pound gorillas.

The silliest example of this is the disappearance of the word "problem." It's forbidden to bring it up in meetings as if the mere mention of a *problem* would frighten and confuse people enough to thrash about and bark like the man-apes of *2001*, who woke up to find an obelisk in their camp. But call it an "opportunity" or a "challenge," and people will respond with "action items", which themselves used to be called, "things to do". Below are some favorite newspeak-to-English translations.

ENGLISH	NEWSPEAK
Problem	Opportunity
Client	Stakeholder
Employee	Associate
Clerk	Subject Matter Expert
Temp	Resource
Computer	Solution
To Do List	Action Items
Something to do	Actionable
Work	Deliverables
Big	Scaleable

Newspeak is a byproduct of the systemic unwillingness to engage in direct communication and confrontation. As long as we're unable to speak our minds, we will continue to invent new ways to *not* speak it.

R.I.P. Conversation

If you don't believe that direct communication is dead, walk through the cubicle floors of any Fortune 500 financial, consulting, or software firm's corporate HQ. Take a listen. What do you hear? That's right. Silence. No phones ringing and no conversation. "Hello Darkness, My Old Friend."

People have simply stopped talking in the workplace. Conversation is dead. There is communication, but it's through instant message or emails. This is a shame, because the work place isn't as much fun without chatter. I miss people talking about the little day-to-day stuff like making fun of each other's haircuts, talking about what was on TV, and even the occasional "F-bomb."

It's all gone thanks to email and instant messaging. Once people start typing to each other, it becomes a slippery slope. Soon, every communication is electronic. A few years ago it seemed nuts to get an email from the guy ten feet away, or an email in which the body of the text was "thanks." *Why doesn't he just call me?* you'd wonder.

Now, its "Thx" instead of "Thanks" and emails from the person sitting directly behind you are the norm, not the exception. Every thought, no matter how slight, is now deemed worthy of immortalization in print. And if you aren't documenting everything, you could be exposing yourself to trouble. We paper our butts with emails while using them to nail our rivals. Our workdays have become documentation arms races, with everyone keeping tabs on everyone else with email. If you aren't playing Documentation Hold 'Em, you are going to get burned at work, because someone will have something on you.

Not only have we stopped talking, we've begun to use chatroom acronyms at work.

> GTG – Got to go
> TTYL – Talk to you later
> NP – No problem
> LOL – The granddaddy of cyber acronyms. If people laughed out loud as often as they typed this the makers of Prozac, Xanex, Vicodin and Atavan would kill themselves.

WTF is going on? The acronyms are an attempt at efficiency, but conversation as a workplace tool is much more efficient than email. The average white-collar worker types at about 35-60 per minute, but can speak at about 120 wpm. Wow, that's at least twice the output. Companies are actually losing money and productivity by encouraging electronic chatter.

But if people and corporations insist on devaluing conversation and the spoken word, that will only make your new, direct, H.A.G.E.N.–style approach that much more effective.

Direct Communication Takes Practice

So always be direct. If you're uncomfortable at first, practice. Practice on people who can't respond in kind. Domestic servants, Thai massage therapists, babies, or the elderly make ideal test subjects because they don't understand, but will provide eye contact.

Once you're relaxed with the technique, you can bring it into the workplace, where you'll be one of the few in your office who will be comfortable with plain speaking. You'll have a huge advantage over your rivals. You'll be a T-Rex in a room full of tethered goats.

G - Get the Principals Speaking. E - Everyone Else Shuts Up

These two are not redundant but are interdependent. You want to get the principals, the main decision-makers, talking. Some managers like to let their lieutenants play "bad cop" at meetings. This is a recipe for disaster; it encourages the other lieutenants to speak up. As conversations drag on and on, your meetings turn into CSPAN within a matter of minutes.

Meetings become bogged down when lower-echelon attendees have their say. That's because once one plebe speaks, then like howler monkeys they all want to speak. The issues with lower-ranked attendees tend to be more granular and even the tone becomes more emotional. Suddenly, your meeting has become the Jerry Springer show, with you as the host. The meeting begins to move away from its main objective as your lower-tier managers argue over minutia.

Suddenly, the rummies are talking about things like "interfaces," "scalability," or "compatibility issues," while you're trying to talk about money. Their issues are generally annoyance issues, but they can put a scare into the room as their rummy counterparts argue each point.

Think back to any Godfather meeting. Who spoke? Was it Michael or was it Rocco? Was it Vito or was it Tessio? The principals speak. The guys who write the checks, make the money, or sign the papers are the ones who should speak.

So before a meeting, prep your team. Let them know that you're the only one speaking unless the employee is specifically called on. Shutting up the minor players will save you countless hours of meeting time.

There will be employees who will bristle under this restriction. You know who they are. You should already have an eye on them as potential traitors or rivals. These employees use the meeting as their forums to show everyone how smart they are and how dumb you are.

The best way to manage this is to stop inviting them to meetings. Take away what they cherish most in the world: an audience. Without a forum or allies to gripe to, these employees first pout, then fume, then eventually go supernova.

An employee supernova usually involves a one-thousand-word resignation letter, which is always good for a laugh because they read like a cross between a jilted lover's letter and the Unabomber's manifesto. The aggrieved employee spills his/her guts, wonders aloud what went wrong, recaps the good times and the bad while thanking you for the opportunity and expressing his regret, then gives you something like three months' notice.

Which gives you three more months to torture him. Enjoy every second of it.

N - No Meeting Should Last More than Ten Minutes

I'm aware that the meetings in the movies are ten minutes or shorter for continuity's sake. Nobody wants to BE in an hour-long meeting, let alone watch one. But is a ten-minute meeting realistic? If you follow the first four principles, if you've followed *H.A.G.E.*... then is a ten-minute meeting anything more than a remote possibility?

I say yes and, like Everest and the Apollo missions, it's something all men should strive for. It should be attempted, because it's never been done...*because it's there.*

A lot of people think a ten-minute meeting is a physical impossibility, like warp speed, the "shrink ray," or universal cellular coverage. They say it's an unattainable absolute. These are the same people who scoffed at the idea of a four-minute mile or a Chinese center in the NBA.

Watch Michael and Frankie Pentangeli go at it in *Godfather II.* From Michael's "Clemenza promised the Rosatto Brothers..." to Frankie's "Cicci, the door," the entire encounter takes place in two minutes, forty-seven seconds.

Think about that. Two minutes and forty-seven seconds. These men were talking about matters of life and death. Crime. Drugs. Violence. Two minutes and forty-seven seconds. And if these kinds of issues can get addressed in under three minutes, why can't you do your meetings in ten? Do you really need an hour to talk about "solutions-driven" focus? Does anyone?

The Gettysburg Address was between two and three minutes long. Granted, Lincoln was a genius, and a mark of genius is the ability to phrase complex issues concisely and memorably for the rest of us to understand.

- "E = mc^2," Albert Einstein
- "Four score and seven years ago..." Abraham Lincoln.
- "Cicci, the door," Frankie Pentangeli.

Both Frankie Five Angels and Lincoln shared the gift of brevity. So it's time to raise the bar, slowpoke. Remember, like Vito and Michael, you're aspiring to greatness in your life. In all likelihood, you won't reach greatness, but merely some level of "very goodness". But that will take guts and originality, a little thing military historians like to call "audacity." Caesar had it. Patton had it. Vito had it.

All it takes is ten minutes to see if YOU have it. Go ahead and hold a ten-minute meeting. I dare you.

Applied H.A.G.E.N.-omics

Let's review the points of H.A.G.E.N. as applied to some of the more memorable meetings in GF1 and GF2. The successful meetings tend to hit all of the points, while the less successful meetings tend to waggle a bit from true H.A.G.E.N.-ism.

1. **The Heads of the Five Families Meet:** This summit is Vito's last great moment in the saga and, like Churchill at Yalta, though older and weaker, he's more than up to the task.

   - **H - Have a firm objective:** The objective of this meeting was to **end a war.** Pretty clear and understandable. No scope creep here.
   - **A – Always be direct:** Vito was direct and diplomatic. Classic Vito, he manages to be threatening and amiable.
   - **G - Get the principals speaking:** Four speakers is just about reaching tolerance levels for H.A.G.E.N.-style meetings. Bonus points if you remember the one head of his family who didn't speak (answer: Cunio).
   - **E – Everyone else shuts up:** Someone named Stracci gets up and pounds a table. He's entertaining, but pointless. Other than that, they all stayed quiet. Especially Cunio.
   - **N - No meeting should last more than ten minutes:** As always, adherence to H.A.G.E. makes the N. possible.

This meeting is brisk and dramatic. You don't get to be one of the heads of the five families without a clear understanding of how to hold a meeting. Imagine, though, if this meeting were held with modern sensibilities, complete with useless handouts like below.

1951   Meeting of the Heads of the Five Families
Executive Room, The Waldorf Astoria, New York

- Welcome from Don Vito Corleone
- Roundtable Discussion: "How Did Things Get So Far?"
- Team Exercise: Vendettas? Should There Be Any?
- 11:30 Lunch - Victor Stracci Presents "Controlling the Drug Trade"
- 1:00 - 5:00 Resolutions, Votes, and Embraces (Have your cameras ready!)
- 6:30 Ladies' Cocktail Party—Meet the *REAL* Heads of the Five Families (The wives host a cocktail reception in the Atrium.)
- Raffle for a brand new territory!
- Dance the Night Away With The Johnny Fontaine Orchestra

2. **Senator Pat Geary Meets with Michael to Discuss Gaming License**: This meeting also tells us all we need to know about Michael as CEO. He's a lot less touchy-feely than Vito, but out of necessity. He's younger and gets treated like a kid by the senator, Frankie Pentangeli, and Hyman Roth.

   - **H - Have a firm objective:** The senator's objective was to "squeeze" Michael. Colorful, yet firm as a military mattress.
   - **A – Always be direct:** Within minutes, these two know exactly where they stand. Geary

forfeits a few points by letting his feelings about Mafia be known. It's direct, but it's too emotional. Keep emotions bottled up during meetings—self-medicate afterwards if you have to.

- **G - Get the principals talking:** Hagen, the Archduke of Restraint, gives Michael a look that says, "Here we go again," but keeps his mouth shut.
- **E – Everyone else shuts up:** The entourages are blissfully silent.
- **N - No meeting should last more than ten minutes:** "Love Me Do" was longer than this meeting that set so many people and events in motion.

3. **Sollozzo "the Turk" meets Vito Corleone:** The Turk is a new kind of animal in the 1950s underworld menagerie—a drug lord. This makes him a dangerous partner and a lethal foe. Vito uses a firm but avuncular approach to deal with Sollozzo.

- **H – Have a firm objective:** Sollozzo's objective is to become partners with Vito. One million dollars gets Vito a franchise in McSolazzo's corp. This may seem cocky, but he respects Vito's time by getting right to the point.
- **A – Always be direct:** Sollozzo's direct, but, at some point, sounds like he's winging it.
- **G – Get the principals talking:** Vito and the Turk engage amicably and directly. Not enough time for anyone to really savor the anisette.

- F – Everyone else shuts up: Sonny goes rogue in this meeting, speaking up and earning Vito's scorn.
- **N – No meeting should last more than ten minutes**: Once again, a pivotal meeting that sets a cataclysm of events in motion is no longer than a Herman's Hermits song.

4. **Viva Las Meetings—Michael Corleone Meets Mo Green:** This is Young Michael's first big meeting sitting in the captain's chair and he acquits himself well against an accomplished veteran, Mo Green a man who made his bones when Michael was dating cheerleaders. Doing the math in my head, I'd say that they Mo made his first bone right around when Mike was eighteen.

   - **H – Have a strong objective**: Per Michael, "The Corleone Family wants to buy you out." So strong it almost made Mo's dice shrivel.
   - **A – Always be direct**: Mo's direct, but he's caught off-guard. *Mo had no objective.* He was there to schmooze, pass out chips, show tickets, and comp buffet vouchers. If he had been prepared, he might have been more receptive to selling out and maybe moving to somewhere like Laughlin or Branson to start another casino town.
   - **G – Get the Principals Talking**: Fredo comes to Mo's defense over the cocktail waitress banging/face-slapping incident. He gets scolded,

memorably, but Michael loses points for not prepping Fredo and for not shushing him in the meeting.

- **E – Everyone else shuts up:** Both principals do the H.A.G.E.N. thing by ignoring Fredo.
- **N – No meeting goes longer than ten minutes:** Michael gets only three drags out of his lit Camel before the meeting finishes up.

The Michael Model for Non-Negotiation Meetings

In this meeting, Michael doesn't so much negotiate as he does dictate. The only choices Mo really has here are:

1. Accept Michael's offer
2. Die

The most common meetings we have week to week are meetings where one party is dictating to another. The boss calls a meeting to tell us about a new compliance regulation. We sit and listen. There is no real negotiation going on.

If you're a boss rolling out your policy change or notification, ask yourself, "is the new policy really open to discussion? Is there anything my staff can say that will change this directive?" If the answer is "no" then tailor your presentation along the Michael Model. Simply dictate, then leave.

Dictate the policy and end the meeting without a Q&A period. Any Q&A increases the risk that you'll be challenged on your wisdom or reasoning by some smart-alecky employee. There are three potentially bad outcomes here:

a. He looks smarter than you because his idea is better.
b. You look weak because you can't justify your policy or explain it.
c. You slam the door on his question and look like a tyrant.

Versus the one good outcome:

d. You answer his question honestly and look like a great manager.

If anyone does have *genuine* questions about implementing the policy, you can tell them to see you in your office after the meeting.

During a Michael model meeting, your employees' choices become Mo's choices, namely, "like it" or "leave." They'll ultimately appreciate your ability to simplify things for them.

5. **Tom Hagen vs. Mr. Woltz—Hagen Does H.A.G.E.N.:** In this one, Tom shows us how it's done. Here Tom has an impressive showing against an old-time studio mogul, leaving Woltz standing there with a bemused look on his face.

- **H – Have a strong objective:** Tom wants Johnny in the picture. Woltz doesn't. It seems like they dawdle a little bit, but this was Hollywood, where the rules were a little different: No doing battle when at least one participant is wearing a tennis outfit.
- **A – Always be direct:** Tom listens while Woltz rants and raves. Listening is an important

communication skill. Ranting is an important skill. Woltz is a classic Hollywood studio king, meaning eighty percent of his day was spent yelling, "It stinks! I hate it." He is a bully but Tom never loses his cool.

- **G – Get the principals talking:** There were no other participants. I'm sure the horse would have liked to have some input.
- **E – Everyone else shuts up.**
- **N – No meeting should last more than ten minutes:** This one clocks in with all the scenes with Woltz coming in at three minutes. In three minutes' time, the fates of Johnny Fontaine and the horse, Khartoum, were decided.

Note: It's impossible to overestimate the visceral impact that the horse's head scene had on 1972 theater audiences. Along with Lon Cheney's unmasking in *Phantom of the Opera*, the shower scene in *Psycho*, and the twisting head in *The Exorcist*, this was one of the most shocking scenes ever filmed.

Some Additional Thoughts on H.A.G.E.N.-ism.

- **Meeting Objective Versus Meeting "Reason":** A meeting objective and a meeting reason are two different things. A "reason" is often the lie or excuse to call the meeting. The objective is the key take-away. A classic example is the peace conference between Frankie and the unnamed Rosatto brother. Rosatto's *reason* is to make a deal. His objective? To assassinate Frankie. Next time you receive a meeting request, try to deduce what the sender's objective is. And if you're the sender, decide on your objective; then, if it helps, camouflage it with a reason.

- **Always Being Direct Doesn't Mean "Always Be Honest":** You can be direct without being honest. Directness, clarity, brevity can have nothing to do with honesty. "I love you" is the quintessential direct lie. Simple, brief, yet sometimes false.

- **Getting the Principals Talking and Everyone Else Shutting Up:** Make sure your employees understand how important this one is to you. If they do speak up and derail a meeting, pull them aside immediately afterwards and suggest that their next meeting will be around a flaming smudge pot under a freeway overpass.

- **No Meeting Should Last More than Ten Minutes:** Like the state of Nirvana is for a Buddhist, the ten-minute meeting should always be your goal. But after years of hour-plus gabfests, you might need to ease into it. Toward this end, start booking shorter meeting times. Forty-five minutes instead of an hour. Thirty minutes instead of forty-five.

People will start to attend your meetings, loving the way you rush through them like a night court judge. You can squeeze in more meetings since yours will be the ones where things actually get accomplished. Once you use H.A.G.E.N., things will start to HAPPEN.

* * *

13. Easy Lies the Head— Lying the Corleone Way

A 1996 SURVEY DONE BY THE UNIVERSITY OF VIRGINIA SUGGESTED THAT PEOPLE LIE AN AVERAGE OF TEN TIMES PER WEEK. On average, each person lied just over ten times, and only seven out of 147 participants claimed to have been "completely honest." Of course, lying about their honesty is one of the most common lies people tell. Having spent twenty-plus years in corporate America, where lies are about as commonplace as fluorescent lighting or paper jams, these numbers seemed kind of low to me.

Why do people lie? Because there is money in it. Because lying will help you make more of it, or keep other people from taking some of yours. *People lie in the workplace to gain a material or tactical advantage.* A zookeeper would have very little incentive to lie in the workplace. What kind of advantage would he gain over a lesser Kudu if he lied to him about the price of oats? On the other hand, a disreputable plastic surgeon has all sorts of incentive to lie.

> "You'll look beautiful!"
> "It won't hurt at all."
> "You'll be back on your feet in a week."

The plastic surgeon is lying to gain a **material** advantage. If the plastic surgeon didn't lie—if he told you how much it would hurt, or that you might end up looking like a mannequin from *A Clockwork Orange*—he wouldn't sell as many surgeries. People wouldn't take the risk.

Lies: Corleone Style

Lying is a fact of life in the workplace, and the Corleones' mastery of the art of lying and lie detection gave them a huge edge in their industry. Deception was the Corleone weapon of choice—intimidation and violence are only last resorts. The big, brutal massacres made for some splashy headlines in the Godfather universe and some great scenes, but deception and misdirection were the tactics of choice and the grease that lubed the Corleone commercial engine. Most of the Corleone mistruths revolved around gaining a **tactical** advantage—to gain power by weakening an opponent.

Deception. Misdirection. Lying. Lie detection. The Corleones and their best rivals had a gift for it. The entire Corleone empire was conceived from a lie: the seminal Vito-Tessio-Clemenza meeting (or the Spaghetti Summit of 1909).

The Corleones played for bigger stakes than we do. Their lies were more outrageous, more cold-blooded. Whereas Michael was lying over whether he killed someone or not, you or I will lie about why we are late every Monday. But, as always, there are lessons and techniques we can take away from watching the Corleones in action, even if we work on a much smaller scale.

Hyman and Michael: Clash of the Titans

The Michael and Hyman encounters of GF2 were the equivalent of a heavyweight title fight with a couple of prevarication pugilists throwing haymakers while lying for their lives. Watch the calm and controlled body language of both men. With everything on the line, neither one so much as blinks in the heat of battle.

This was more than a couple of sociopaths lying out of survival instinct. This was genius-level misdirection, practiced and perfected by two demigods of deception. Each lie was a shining example of the art. Some of the multi-faceted gems they displayed were:

- Michael saying he just wants to "wait" a little longer before investing in Havana. In reality, he needs to buy time to keep Hyman from figuring out the true end game: that Michael wants to kill him.
- Hyman, meanwhile, talking about his "sixth sense" regarding Fredo's big bag of cash, is pretending to be anxious about closing a big deal for the both them, when in reality he's got a midnight deadline to kill Michael and steal his two million dollars.
- Earlier, Michael told Hyman he thought Pentangeli tried to kill him. Michael was trying to sell Hyman on the idea that he didn't blame Hyman himself.
- Hyman, meanwhile, is trying to control his glee that he nearly killed Michael and, now, Michael is going to knock off one of his rivals for him.

These two were so good, so subtle, that even when we watch the movie and know the outcome, we still can't tell if they're lying or not. In fact, to be honest, I had no idea what the heck was going on in this movie the first three times I watched it, yet I loved it nonetheless.

These two crossed swords for nearly half the movie, and we can't help but admire their skill with a blade. Lying is a sort of "dark art" and if you don't want to practice it then, like a student at Hogwart's, you should at least be able to defend yourself against its nefarious effects and be able to recognize it.

Is it possible to make it big in the workplace without lying? Possibly, if you're a zookeeper or pre-school teacher.

Keep your friends close, but your shirt on. Letterboxed liars Hymen Roth and Michael Corleone went toe-to-toe. (Lee Strasburg and Al Pacino in *The Godfather Part II,* Paramount Pictures, 1974)

Tallest Godfather Tales—The "Whoppers"

For your pleasure, here is a list of some of the greatest lies in *Godfather* mythology. Lies so big that you can't help but admire the cannoli of the person spinning it.

1. **Michael tells Kaye he didn't kill Carlo (GF1):**
   Let's give Kaye some credit. It takes guts to ask your husband if he killed your brother-in-law, especially in front of the movers. This was bad timing for Michael, too, as Kaye and Connie bust in on him at a moment when, with cigarette hanging from his lips, his hair slicked back ala Dillinger, and his mouth agape in a menacing maw, he had a strangely inhuman expression. In other words, he looks, well, kind of guilty. The only way he could have looked worse was if he had flecks of blood on his face or Carlo's head in a jar.

2. **Michael tells Connie he didn't kill Carlo (GF1):**
   Michael takes the top two spots. Moments before confronting Kaye with the number one lie, Michael warmed up on Connie. Technically, Michael didn't really lie here. Some other guy "killed" Carlo. He hugged Connie to ease her "hysteria." It was an awkward-looking move and if he had to do it all over again, I'm sure he would have given her some Klonapin first before moving in for the embrace.

3. **Michael tells Carlo he won't kill…Carlo (GF1):**
   Completing an impressive trifecta, these scenes send a chill up the viewer's spine. Michael's ability to lie blatantly illustrated his remorselessness. In fact,

remorse never lays a glove on Michael until about two hours and fifty minutes into GF2.

4. **Sonny puts Paulie at ease after his role in Vito's hit (GF1):** When a guy like Sonny gives you special attention and care, it's time to get in your Packard and drive as fast as you can toward the Canadian border. In business, be on the lookout when a supervisor who hates your guts suddenly loves your work. Your papers have likely been filed with HR and a severance check is being cut.

5. **Michael tells Congress he's not a criminal (GF2):** Fans often speculate about the falling out between Tom and Michael, but I think it may have a little to do with Tom's performance here as Michael's defense attorney, which nearly ended in five counts of perjury for Michael. Was it Tom who advised, "Don't bother with pleading the Fifth. They've got nothing. In fact, I think you should open with a self-righteous statement." After this sorry showing, you couldn't blame Michael if he took a little off of Tom's plate, or gave him some easier legal dealings, like probate or easement issues.

6. **Vito tells Clemenza and Tessio his plan to negotiate with Fanucci (GF2):** Vito's real plan was to kill Fanucci. As mentioned earlier, deception is the weapon of choice for Vito and this meeting is his "discovery of fire" moment. It gave him all the advantages. A few years later, he's sitting on top of the world, with a respectable little moustache to boot.

7. **Vito tells Don Fanucci he's running a little short (GF2):** Vito hands Fanucci only $100, which means

he didn't even kick in his share of the payoff. That takes real audacity. Fanucci was right about one thing: that kid Vito was going places.

8. **Hyman speaks to the press at the airport before his murder (GF2):** Granted, everyone lies to the press and the press lies about what everyone says. In this case, Hyman wanted to live out his golden years in Israel, telling the press he was "a retired investor living on a pension." Minutes later, the "living" part of that sentence ceased to be true as well.

9. **Hyman tells Michael that they are bigger than U.S. Steel (GF2):** Financial reports suggest that even with adjustments for inflation, Hyman grossly overestimated the combined nets-worth of both men, based on the stock price of U.S. Steel on New Year's Eve 1959. That's OK. He was excited.

10. **Fredo plays dumb in Havana (GF2):** Fredo played dumb the way Roy Hobbs played baseball in *The Natural*. But this was different. This time it was intentional. Fredo was Hyman Roth's man on the inside and had to feign ignorance while he and Michael bonded over banana daiquiris. At some point, there's a look of concern that crosses Michael's face over Fredo's twitchiness. But Fredo managed to convince him it was travel fatigue or "propeller lag."

Lying with Style and Confidence

We all agree that lying is a bad thing. It's bad for your soul. It's bad for your conscience. It's blah, bad, blah, bad, blah. But remember that the workplace is a battlefield. If you were a soldier captured by the enemy, would you feel bad about giving them false information? Your captors would presume that you're lying. Your commanders would expect and commend you for it.

Besides, according to the University of Virginia, you are constantly being lied to an average of ten times a week. Let's face it; it's an arms race of bullshit. You will either need to lie and be better at it than your rivals or you'll need to be better at detecting it than they are. And you'll need to be committed to it. Lying is a little like acting: If you have doubts or equivocations about it, you'll stink at it, and then you'll really have trouble.

There are plenty of reasons to have doubts or equivocations about bending or even breaking, the truth. It's a troubling act. A universally condemned act. It's a sin. Everytime we lie, there's a little part of us that senses God shaking his head sadly, then making a notation next to our name in a cosmic ledger. We all know lots of people that we suspect are liars, and we despise them accordingly. Politicians. Used car salesmen. Mortgage brokers.

Lying is also seen as a slippery slope. Lie once, the conventional wisdom goes, and it becomes easier to do. Once caught in a lie, you may never shake the label. With all this risk associated with the act, is there a more sickening feeling than being caught in a lie? Or having caught a loved one in a lie? We've all caught our children in lies and felt sick with disappointment. It's risky and difficult, but, in business, it's necessary.

So how can you get good at it?

Prevarication for Profit: Just Business

To deceive like a champ, your mind needs to be clear and emotions need to be controlled. Remember chapter 1. The workplace is where you need to be emotionally detached. Guilt is an emotion. Eliminate it or compartmentalize it and you should see an instant improvement in your lies.

The foundation of the Corleone pyramid of strength is the separation of business and personal spaces. This gave them, and us, our core strength and separates us from our competition. We can act brutally, speak bluntly, and accept attacks with inner calm.

The separation of "family" and "workplace" will also help you lie with confidence. We all know that it's hard to lie to your spouse and it's heartbreaking to lie to your children. That's because they are your family. But lying to the schmuck in accounting or the nutty lady in quality control can be easy if you've got your emotions in check. If you're uncomfortable with the term "lying," try "**prevarication for profit.**"

Once you resign yourself to the necessity of lying at work, then you should never lie at home. Not to your children, your spouse, or even your mistress. You have to stick to this one or it won't work. This will also help clear your conscious as you distinguish yourself as a prevaricator and not a common liar.

If work is war, then lying is a weapon of war, and therefore has no place in your home. If you were a soldier, you wouldn't bring your M-16 and prop it up in the kitchen. You wouldn't toss your hand grenades onto an end table as you empty your pockets for the night.

Limiting deception only to the workplace will not only reward you financially, but emotionally as well. Let's face it. It feels good to put one over on someone you really can't stand, or to lie your way out of a jam. Lastly, even though you will lie, do not think or refer to yourself as a liar. Instead you're:

- A tactician keeping the enemy off balance
- An illusionist performing verbal sleight of hand

- A soldier on reconnaissance behind enemy lines
- A diplomat, learning everything he can while saying nothing substantive

That's how Michael and Hyman justified it, and they both slept pretty well at night (Hyman, of course, having to get up to urinate more frequently than Michael).

Practical Tips about Lying

Now that we've given ourselves the moral foundation to deceive with certitude and authenticity, here are some practical tips to help you get better at it. Deception, like anything else, is worth doing right.

1. **Avoid Babble-On**: People telling lies tend to babble on until they get re-enforcement. Would Michael or Vito babble on?
2. **Learn your physiological tells:** Red face, perspiration, dilated pupils, and unusual breathing patterns are typical physiologic tells. A lack of eye contact is sometimes seen as an indication of a lie.
3. **Once again, practice on someone insignificant first:** Domestic servants, very young children, or the elderly make ideal test targets since they are powerless to do anything about it or won't remember anything if they catch you. Even if they confront you, you can use those moments as a dress rehearsal for when you are caught by someone who might matter. This may run counter to the rule of "no lying

to family" but this is just your rehearsal period. Use ridiculous lies ("I was in the space program") and make it fun.

Or make it a game. Tell them five things, one of which is completely false. See if they can spot it.

4. **Don't repeat a direct question:** A person asks you, "Did you read the proposal?" You blurt out, "Did I read the proposal?" out of fear. This is a near-autonomic response, like a pain response, and nearly impossible to control, but it is controllable with some discipline. Watergate co-conspirator and ex-CIA operative G. Gordon Liddy, believing he could control autonomic responses, used to hold his hand directly over a candle flame as a sort of party trick. When asked, "How do you manage to control the pain?" Liddy responded that the trick was not in controlling the pain; the trick was in "not caring about the pain."

You have to teach yourself not to care about lying to your enemies.

5. **Liars assume that you're lying. Use that to your advantage:** Most habitual liars assume that others lie as often as they do. They also think that they are experts at lie detection. You can throw them off your scent by sending off false tells when you are telling the truth.

This is an old poker players' trick, but will work just was well in the boardroom. Try repeating direct questions before answering completely honestly. Or add too much detail. Your rivals will think they have you pegged and that they can tell when you are lying. You can really cash in for some "big pots" with this move if you are patient and cultivate them carefully.

Avoid eye contact. Give too much detail. Repeat the questions. Do it judiciously. It will pay off big one day as they try to call you for lying about something that will turn out to be completely true and easily proven.

6. **Lying creates a need for more lies—the vector of a lie:** Often, a simple, little falsehood needs more falsehoods to back it up—fake alibis, phony timelines, made-up names, receipts, a corpse.

It can all spin out of control rather quickly. Pretty soon you've got something close to an alternate universe on your hands, like when the Terminator went back in time to kill John Connor. Soon even you can't follow what the hell is going on. Tensions rise as it could all blow up with one misstep.

This effect is what I refer to as "vectoring." In physics, a vector is represented by a directional arrow. The vectors of a lie are the people affected or involved, the processes affected, or the factors that need to fall into place for it to work. The more vectors your lie has, the riskier it is to tell. Try diagramming or planning your lie for potential vectors before you tell it. An example of a "lie-a-gram" is below.

Possible Lie:

I couldn't finish my work on time because the system was down.

Vectors:

Joe was able to do his work.
Timestamps show that I went home BEFORE the system crashed
My work was already 3 days late

Vectors and Supporting Lies:

Joe was able to do his work.
   I can ask Joe to submit late?
Timestamps show that I went home BEFORE the system crashed.
   I can mess around with timestamps?
My work was already 3 days late.
   Uh-oh...

Judging by this lie-a-gram, this is a lie with some tough vectors to overcome and little chance of succeeding. The vector "I was already past deadline" in fact, is a critical failure point for this lie. If you are already late on a project, it will be tough to blame your failure on system downtime. For most people, a lie is a product of panic – panic born out of fear of failure, fear of blame. Monst panic lies will have at least one critical failure point. By staying calm and planning your lie before you execute it, you can better analyze your chances of success.

7. **Touch and tell:** A practiced liar is often very touchy-feely. They know that we respond to touch. We lower our guard when touched. We feel loved. That little touch adds a little extra "please" to the "please believe me" emotional subtext of the lie. The picture below shows Vito laying a little touch and tell on the witless Carlo, who's been told he's being "promoted" by Michael and is being "congratulated" by Vito.

After a lifetime of deception, Vito could pull off a lie the way Fred Astaire could bust out a buck-and-wing: effortlessly and with unforgettable style and grace.

So get out there and start lying. If you can get to the point where you can grab a handful of someone's face and tell him or her a complete load of garbage, well, then, you're really on your way!

Common Workplace Lies

You've probably already lied in these situations, but now you should be able to successfully pull it off with much more frequency.

1. **True costs of your products**—This is an easy lie to justify because the axiom, "let the buyer beware," puts the onus on the buyer. To the most ruthless

salesman, that phrase justifies anything in the name of a sale.

2. **True price of something you need**—You need a system, project, asset, or resource, so you lie to your boss about the ultimate cost. When your boss complains about the checks he/she is writing, you make up some soft R.O.I. numbers to justify the cash.

3. **Lengthy timelines**—It's easy to say that something will be done "next month," because we know that so much can change in that time. A month has become like geological time in the workplace. It's so long, it can hardly be envisioned.

4. **Someone's job status**—Your employee asks you if his position is about to be eliminated and you lie to him/her. This is also an easy lie to execute, since it seems almost like an act of kindness, like telling someone they don't look as fat as they are. Mostly, it's just an act of cowardice.

5. **Culpability or blame**—There's a fairly large segment of the population that thinks that admitting to mistakes is a sign of strength. This is completely untrue. **Never, EVER admit to making a mistake in the workplace.** Lie your way out of a mistake. Point fingers in every direction but your own. If you have to, blame it on an ally. If you lose an ally, big deal. If the United States lost Germany as an ally, how long do you think it would have taken before we started building bases in Portugal?

If there is no way to lie your way out of the mistake, then **never apologize for it.** Apologies only amplify the perception of the severity of the mistake.

Shrug the mistake off with "Win some, lose some" or "welcome to the NFL, pal" bravado.

Victimless Lies

There are lies that are not specifically injurious to anyone. No one's reputation gets hurt. Nobody loses any money. These are "victimless" lies. They are often referred to as "little white lies," white being the color of good. Since there is little downside to a victimless lie, feel free to use them whenever applicable. Some examples of business-related victimless lies are:

1. **Cheating on income taxes**—There is a victim here (the U.S. government), but I think they can take care of themselves.

2. **Delivery dates on low-priority work**—If you ever get called to the mat, you can say you were focused on the high-priority stuff. Nobody gets hurt. If you sell it right, you can come off looking dedicated.

3. **Your salary**—There are times when it will benefit you to low-ball your salary, and other times when the right move will be to exaggerate it. Let's try a practice exercise: You are being wined and dined by a likeable, slick sales manager who makes three times what you do. This particular likeable, slick sales manager can make that kind of money because he is willing to throw some perks or kickbacks at potential clients.

Should you:

A)   downplay your salary in the hopes that he'll see you as desperate for a sweetener? or

B)   exaggerate your salary so that he knows you're a player?

The answer is B). If you underplay your salary, he's less likely to offer a kickback. He'll assume that you're the kind of guy who makes decisions based on things like "delivery dates" or "service levels" or "facts," and he'll be right. He might even assume that someone like you would look down on a bribe. So why waste the money on you?

So when the likable, slick sales manager takes you out to dinner, you should look like a person who really likes money: Wear your best suit and invest $3.95 in a copy of *Yachting* magazine or *Forbes* and keep it tucked under your arm.

4.   **Email timestamps**—Using a timestamp on your email is a great way to lie about your productivity. Nothing says "dedication" like a lengthy email with a 7:34 p.m. timestamp. These days we're wired to a greater degree than ever so there are all sorts of opportunities to show the boss how often you're thinking about work through judicious time stamping.

The risk here is that your boss is very likely pulling the same trick on his boss. But when done with panache, this little maneuver can make you a fortune. The trick is to keep it fresh and mix up your pitches. Vary your times and days. Try to match the tone of the email with the time and day to get a more authentic feel.

For example, if you are sending the email Thursday night from the office, use your professional and polished tone. "Polished and professional tone" means:

- Lots of bullet points
- Issues only
- Sub-headings like "Action Items"
- Put dates on things

It helps if you make a "grouchy" or focused face. That expression and emotion will permeate the email.

If you are sending one Saturday morning from home, try a breezy, casual subject line like "Thinking about what you said...." The breezier tone is acceptable because you are in your home. Make sure you use the "..." punctuation. This is the literary equivalent of a daydream—a sentence trailing off.

These are also the emails where it's okay to use "smileys" or emoticons such as, "Sylvia should be really happy when she sees the new revisions;)."

Sign off with a little personal note about your plans for the rest of the weekend—something that projects an image. For example: "OK. Gotta run. Going to take the kids to the park and fly kites." It reminds the reader of the sacrifice you've made this particular

Saturday, while demonstrating that you're a laidback and dedicated family guy.

Who doesn't want one of *those* on his team?

Why go on about smileys and timestamps and "..."? Because the right kind of details in the right amounts can make the difference between a profitable lie and a libel suit. Even with victimless lies, you should cover your tracks as best you can.

Cinema Verite: Creating Colorful and Authentic Lies.

Imagine that your lie is a movie. You're not only the writer and director of that movie, you're also the special effects artist. Don't discount anything that will give your "movie" authenticity. Authenticity is what Francis Ford Coppola infused into *The Godfather* saga to make the every moment completely believable and indelible. Even the most fantastic set pieces (the horse's head in the Hollywood bed, the Baptism massacres, the perforation of Sonny) all have an unmistakable stamp of HISTORY. It's all fiction, yet every moment of the movie feels as if we are looking directly into a genuine past.

How did he do it?

Part of it is just magic. With *The Godfather Part I,* Coppola brought something completely new to the screen. He gave us reality, without any "grittiness." It was beautiful and ghastly and absolutely genuine. At the time of its release, no movie had ever looked this rich or this real. And like Sgt. Peppers, it somehow seems as fresh and original today as it did thirty-seven years ago.

The other part was good old-fashioned attention to detail—the sweaty sheen of Clemenza's skin, the bulging eyes of Luca

13. Easy Lies the Head—Lying the Corleone Way

Brasi in his death throes, Sonny's T-shirt. Perfection lay in the details.

So should it be with your lie—your *movie*. If you're telling a story about an argument you had, why not splash some water on your face, to look either overheated, or like someone trying to cool off? If you're going to tell your boss you worked all night to fix the presentation (when in reality you went home by seven) make sure you wear yesterday's shirt.

Getting in the right emotional frame of mind will help too. Like an actor rehearsing a role, try to experience your lie before you tell it. If you're spinning a yarn about how you told a vendor off, put yourself in an agitated frame of mind. Imagine the conversation. Play it out in your head. Get yourself riled up. Then yell "ACTION" and storm in and start lying.

Just remember not to yell "Cut!" when you're done. It will raise some eyebrows.

* * *

Remember your newfound proficiency at lying is a sort of superpower. *You must use that power only for EVIL and never for GOOD.* That's not backwards. In other words, use it at **WORK** and never use it at **HOME.**

* * *

14. Out of the Mailroom: Godfatherly Advice for Beginners

MOST OF THE CONCEPTS IN THIS BOOK WERE TAILORED FOR MIDDLE MANAGERS OR CORPORATE VETERANS. Negotiation, meeting facilitation, decision-making, or lying, these are usually the tasks and tools of middle managers, analysts, and the like. But for those of you starting in the mailroom, or at Kinko's, or about to make your first foray into the workplace, you'll reap rewards aplenty from an enlightened viewing of the *Godfather* saga (assuming that you can afford the DVDs).

Remember that the story of Vito Corleone is a rags-to-riches story, straight out of Horatio Alger or old-time Broadway.

Boy is born poor!

Boy's parents are killed by Mafia chieftain!

Boy hides in donkey cart and makes his way to the Big Apple!

Boy marries girl. Gives girl a pear! Steals girl a rug!

Boy kills local Mafia boss, grows moustache and turns the town on its ear!

Vito arrived with nothing to his name, not even his own name. Remember that Vito's name was changed to *Corleone* by Ellis Island clerks, who for some reason, had trouble processing certain immigrant names, even though they saw thousands of immigrants a day. Maybe they did it to break up the day. Luckily, the Ellis Island clerk wasn't a prankster, and he gave Vito a perfectly serviceable name, *Corleone*, instead of *Hootie* or *Picklejar.*

He landed in a hellish environment, turn-of-the-century New York, and managed to work his way to the top. If he can do it, without any education, language skills, or even PARENTS, then you can do it too. So whether you're in crime (like Vito) or IT or retail, there are certain things you can do to get your career off on the right track.

The basic ideas behind the book, emotional control, lying for profit, Vito-based decision making, and so on, also apply to starter positions. Business is business no matter how low you are. Learn them and live them and you'll be one-step ahead of your fellow sardines.

Here are some extra pointers that can give you an extra edge as you fight your way upstream.

Personal Metrics: The Age / Salary Goal

This is a simple metric for measuring your progress in your career. Your salary should equal your age times one thousand dollars.

So if you are twenty-two years old, you should be making at least $22,000. If you are thirty, you should be making $30,000. When I first used this goal, I was twenty-year-old college dropout making $12,000/year. Keeping that number in mind pushed me to hustle and fight to get ahead. For myself, it was a great motivator as I fought my way to positions of increasing responsibility and pay

Position	Salary
Front Office Manager	$22,000/year
Customer Support Tech.	$28,000/year
Systems Manager	$42,000/year
Director, Quality Control	$60,000/year
Systems Consultant	$71,000/year
Project Manager	$88,000/year
COO, Software Startup	$650.18 entire year
Help Desk Tech.	$36,000/year
Asst. Vice President	$102,000/year

Sure there were some bumps in the road, like the years between project manager and assistant vice president when I tried to start my own software company two years after the E-commerce bubble had burst. I had to start at the bottom after a year and half out of the job market.

But Vito and me, well, we somehow always manage to claw our way back.

Brown Nosing: A Young Man's (or Woman's) Game

Brown-nosing, has become part of the business lexicon. But because "brown-nosing" implies *sticking your nose so far into the anus of a superior that your nose comes out with a brown fecal tinge,* it can have some negative connotations, and you might find it objectionable.

But brown-nosing when you are young and starting out is not nearly as egregious as when you are established and older. In fact, it's kind of endearing to your bosses, the person whose anus you'll be inserting your nose into. Here are some tips on better brown-nosing.

- **Refer to your boss often as a "mentor":** They get a kick out of it, and it brings out something paternal/maternal in them. Calling some poor has-been of a boss a "mentor" will make him your ally for life.

- **Try to make a personal connection:** Become fans of his favorite college team. Buy and read something that you spied on his shelf. If he/she has pictures of young children on his desk, tell him how cute they are and ask their names and ages (unless his/her kids are high school age. Then steer clear)

- **Try to refrain from talking about yourself:** As a middle-aged man with kids, a mortgage, a bad back, and all sorts of grown-up problems, I can tell you that there is nothing we middle-aged guys with bad backs and problems at home find more tiresome than hearing about the "problems" of a twenty-something.

  Don't talk to your managers about your girl-friend / boyfriend problems, or how your new condo doesn't have a good place for an entertainment center, or how your puppy chewed up your stuffed animals, or how it's really hard to find time fit in your regular gym workout with this new high-paying job we just gave you. Remember you are talking to guys who consider taking the stairs instead of the elevator to buy a bag of Doritos at the vending machine an effort tantamount to scaling K2. When you whine about problems that we would love to have, we write you off as inconsequential.

- **Ask about us instead:** Ask for our advice. Ask us how we got "ahead". Be quiet and listen. Those are the kinds of young people we like to be around. And if you can put up with our repetitive, self-serving success stories, like the one about how the department was a disaster until we got here, then you will impress us and we will take you under our wing.

Personal Habits

In the early days, there is little you can control about your job or your environment. You are beginning to come to grips with the fact that you are a nobody. Your ideas aren't listened to and your work has little impact. But during this time you should strive to make your own personal habits and behaviors beyond reproach. It takes time, but people eventually notice someone who's got their act together.

- **Don't be late for anything:** Never ever arrive late for a meeting. When you arrive late for a meeting, there are ten to twelve witnesses. You've just sent a message to a room full of people that you're stupid and can't keep time. Also, never ever wander in late for work with a **hangover**. Coming in while still tipsy but *on time*, is preferable than being late with a hangover. There's almost something admirable to the latter.

- **Dress like Vito would if he had meaningless job like yours:** Even when Vito couldn't afford a pot to piss in, or a decent pear for his wife, he dressed like a winner. Clean, modest, trim, and professional. Find that look in a magazine and emulate it. If you don't know anything about clothes, your rule for buying them should be the same as with shoes. *If the price of a shirt makes you say, "Holy crap. I'm not paying THAT for a shirt" then that is the shirt you should buy.*

- **Don't gain weight at work:** If you have put on ten to fifteen pounds since starting work, knock it off right away. A person who gains weight on the job is rightfully seen as overstressed, overwhelmed, and undisciplined. Regardless of whether you are already heavy, weight gain on the job is a sign of weakness. It says "The job is getting the better of you." This has nothing to do with how big or thin you are when you start. In other words, it's OK to be big when you start. Your own body image is the most important factor. But *gaining* weight at work will stigmatize you.

Soft Soap Your Threats

Eventually, your Vito-like behaviors and work ethic are going to get you noticed and promoted. As you escape the crushing gravity of the mailroom, the motor pool or the House of Representatives, remember to stay humble. Now that you've got a taste of power and responsibility, you have license to lean on your former colleagues. But tread lightly. You want to keep everyone an ally if possible. That's the easiest way to continued success.

Take a page out of Vito's playbook and use a gentle approach. Instead of threatening, let them know that you're the kind of person who knows how to repay a favor. It's right from Vito's mouth, and the subtle implication is that you are also the kind of person who knows how to "repay" an insult or refusal.

When I was a systems administrator, I asked a purchasing director if he could place a critical order for me without the necessary signatures. It was a systems related emergency. I would get the approvals later or the next day, but I needed the supplies today. He refused me this service. I told him I would really appreciate it, just this once, and appealed to him in my most magnanimous, "Vito speaking-to-the-landlord," tone of voice.

He refused to bend. So I turned off his phone lines, disabling them from my magic systems console. In the days before the Web, a purchasing director without a phone or fax was like an air traffic controller without a radar or cocaine. He knew it was me and from a pay phone across the street, he threatened to go to the G.M. if I didn't' turn on his phones. I said I was sorry for his troubles, that I would look into the problem as soon as possible, but I couldn't now because I was too busy chasing down signatures for my requisition. But if he could manage to forego the signatures on the requisition, then I would be able to focus properly on this annoying phone issue.

Sure enough, he saw the light, and moments later, his phones were happily ringing off the hook again.

It's nice when things work themselves out like this.

* * *

15. Vito Implementation Plan

So now you understand why you're emotional and will work hard to control it. Like the Corleones, you'll be able to lay some wood on some people and feel okay about it. Your new insights and self-worth will translate into better communication skills, both verbal and non-verbal. Gone is the twitchy, nervous, yammering ninny, who was always looking over his shoulders. People will sense the change in you and start yammering and chattering at you for a change.

When faced with a tough decision, you'll "run it by Vito in your head," with WWVD. If you are a Fredo, you'll cancel your appointment with the medical marijuana doctor and schedule some serious psychotherapy. If you're a Sonny, you're going to manage your temper while keeping your pizzazz. If you're a Tom, you'll ask yourself if it's time to move up, move on, or stay where you are. If people are treating you funny, you'll know that it's because the presence of an extremely strong second in command can be a distraction, and not because you're bald.

For you Michaels, a little dose of humility, warmth and caring, even phony baloney caring will go a long way for you. Remember that your talents and your intelligence make you a threat to some people and that, if they catch a whiff of arrogance from you, they will make it their mission in life to take you down.

If you make a mistake, never apologize for it. It may be the *right* thing to do, but it's also a *stupid* thing to do. People will lie to you, but you'll be better at sniffing it out. You might have to lie back, but it won't tear you apart inside. Work is where you have to fight to survive. When it's time to lie, you'll know how to make it more convincing.

It's a lot to learn and you may wonder how to keep it all straight. The chapter outline can be a good implementation guide. Starting with controlling your emotions will give you the clarity to improve your communication skills, to understand that you're in a fight for your life, to reclassify your relationships, to make better decisions via WWVD, and so on.

Below, we present the ideas in a more visual format along the lines of other famous graphical touchstones like the famous "food pyramid" or the national terror alert color scale. We call it "Clemenza's Sauce of Success."

Sauce of Success

In *The Godfather Part I,* Clemenza teaches Michael how to make sauce, starting with the foundation, then adds more and more hearty, flavorful ingredients. "You start with a little bit of oil, and you fry some garlic." He doesn't give us any proportions or times. But he then tells Michael to throw in some "tomatoes, tomato paste...you fry it to make sure it doesn't stick."

Clemenza isn't a technician. He's an artist. He doesn't say "how much" or "how long," but he does know the order of things. Sequencing is everything.

1. **Emotional Control - (start out with a little bit of oil).** Emotional control is the foundation of the sauce of success. Without it, you won't be able to execute any other steps.

2. **Improve your communications (you throw in some garlic).** Another important foundation step. If you can't effectively communicate, you'll have emotional control and little else. Remember that the Corleone's always took the most direct route when it came to communications. No corporate speak. No equivocation. This is garlic, after all. It should be strong and pungent

3. **Identify Allies, Rivals and Traitors (throw in some tomatoes, tomato paste – make sure it doesn't stick).** Like Clemenza's sauce, this is the step where things get flavorful. With your emotional control and clarity of thought, it will be that much easier to spot the good guys and bad guys in your life. Monitor your relationships closely. Re-classify them from time to time. Like the tomatoes and tomato paste, this step takes a little bit of work.

4. **What Would Vito Do? (shove in all your sausage and your meatballs).** This step is the "meat" of our methodology. You want to be able to act, think and decide like Vito.

5. **Which Corleone Are You? (add a little bit a' wine).** Executing the foundation ingredients in order, you can now get more subtle. Finding out which Corleone you are gives you the luxury of introspection, which will help you avoid some of your past mistakes.

6. **Lying with Authenticity / H.A.G.E.N meetings (add some sugar – that's my trick).** With an understand of who you are, and with the strong

foundation established in sections 1-4, you'll be able to lie like a champ in some tough spots. Even better, that clarity will help you sniff out the amateurish lies flung around by your rivals. You'll also be able to take a forceful stand at your meetings, bringing them to speedy and decisive conclusions.

Dip a nice piece of Italian bread into that my friend and *mangia* on some tasty success. It will taste a lot sweeter than what you're munching on now. In the sauce scene, Sonny scolds Clemenza saying he "has more important things for him to do." But notice how closely Michael pays attention. In his mind, he's already made the connection between sauce and life.

* * *

As with anything important in life (sauce, lasagna, zuppa di mare) you get out of it what you put into it. It's not enough to add the right ingredients in the right sequence. The missing ingredient, is love.

Love of what you do. Love of yourself and your family. Love of sauce. With the information and diagrams in the book, you have the blueprint to Corleone type success and contentment. But if you don't love what you do then love *who you are doing it for,* otherwise no amount of personal control, WWVD, or tomato paste is going to make it right.

Not even clams will help

The best career advice for anyone is to do what you love for a living. That way it doesn't feel like work. But if you can't do what you love, and work is making you miserable, then try doing it The Godfather Way. You may never end up loving what you do, you most likely will never live your dreams, but by fighting back against the bullies, liars, and cheats, by ridding yourself of a few bad apples, by discovering an inner strength you never knew you had, you might find it a little easier to swallow.

Vito Corleone wasn't living his dream. He didn't aspire to be a "hood." Things just panned out that way. He made the best of it, and you can too. Many of us work jobs with titles that our parents or kids don't understand like *coordinator for distance learning* or *credit control analyst.* When we were five, we wanted to be firemen, astronauts, teachers, or nurses. At age thirty-five, in this economy, you're lucky to be a credit control analyst. The real world has a way of imposing its will on your dreams, as it did to Vito and Michael. You're not going to be a fireman. Michael was never going to be a senator. Vito was never going to be a respectable businessman.

But, at the end of the day, if you can provide a living for your family, take pride in what you do, stand up for yourself, and take time to stop and smell the sauce by appreciating your family and yourself, then you're doing okay by anybody's book.

* * *

Bonus—The DaVito Code

WHEN MY OLDEST SON TURNED TWELVE, I SAT HIM DOWN
TO INTRODUCE HIM TO *THE GODFATHER* SAGA. This was a moment I had been waiting on since his birth. Sure the birth was
exciting, but this was the real reason I wanted a son in the first
place. I had been waiting to give him this gift. I pulled out
my Coppola edition DVD and announced, "Son, we are going to
watch what is thought by many people to be the greatest movie
ever made. It's at least in the top three on everyone's list." With
the ceremonial solemnity of a Massai king sending his son out
to kill his first lion, or a redneck dad sharing his first beer with
his kid, I sat down to commence this rite of passage.

I popped in the DVD. Thirty minutes later, between the
time Johnny Fontaine made his appearance at the wedding and
Sonny smashed a camera, I caught his eyes wandering. Thirty-
five minutes later, he was politely stifling his yawns. By the
time the wedding scene was over, I had lost him. He got up
and left to play the videogame "City of Villains."

City of Villains, I thought. *But that's what we're watching!*

I blew it, I realized later. I introduced him to it too early.
I grew up the Italian American son of an immigrant. This
movie, after all, was our *Roots*. It was a cultural happening for
us. But there is no way this movie would have the sociological
relevance today that it had then. Being an Italian American
back in 1973, only 1 generation removed from the motherland,

meant being an ITALIAN American. Today, it's more about being Italian AMERICAN.

So I forgave him. But I started to think about the hold the movie still had on my contemporaries and me. There were other landmark movies from the late 60s and early 70s that were poetically violent and dramatically stirring. But we aren't still buzzing about the *French Connection* or *Patton* or *Five Easy Pieces.* We've outgrown *A Clockwork Orange* and *Dr. Strangelove.* *The Godfather* is still ringing in our ears.

I think it's because every moment, every beautifully filmed millisecond of *The Godfather* is framed with subtext and metaphor. There are reasons that Vito is petting a cat in the opening scene, or reasons that the curtains are drawn a certain way. There are reasons Tom's face is half-obscured by shadow as he held by the Turk. First produced in the era of "subliminal seduction," *The Godfather's* hidden secrets hold up beautifully and can be appreciated even more today with DVD freeze framing and constant rewinding. Along with the story and the performances, Coppola and Puzo were speaking to us in a code. Yet the movies are so great that you can completely miss the code and still enjoy the greatest movies of a generation, maybe of all time. But if you catch the symbolism, it's like finding the writing behind the Mona Lisa in *The DaVinci Code.*

So I present to you *The DaVito Code*: the hidden meaning behind select scenes and images in *The Godfather* saga. There have been entire books written on this subject, such as: *Francis Ford Coppola's The Godfather Trilogy* by Cambridge University Professor Nick Brown. I'll go out on a limb and suggest that he's got a little more insight into this stuff than I do. You can choose to believe whether these symbols or hidden messages are real or not. But I do believe that if you let yourself see them (or even *pretend* to see them while watching with your friends), you get more out of some movies that are already giving plenty.

These images and symbols are entirely my own interpretation and haven't been cribbed from any film criticism books or articles (not even the free ones you can get on Google).

- **The Holy Trilogy of *The Godfather, Part I, Part II*, and *Part III*—**Call me crazy, but Part I is the story of "the father, Vito," Part II is the story of "the son, Michael" and Part III? It's about the son's attempt to make his peace with God. It's about Michael trying to find his *holy spirit*. **The Father, The Son, and The Holy Spirit?** Could it really be? The THIRD installment of the series is about the Holy Spirit and which makes the entire saga a metaphor for the Holy Trinity! How cool is that?

- **The White Coat of Don Fanucci—**Why is it that Fanucci was dressed in virginal white, while surrounded by the grit and dirt of the Lower East Side slums? I believe that it was Coppola's intention to show Fanucci as a living ghost—something from the past, an old idea or way of doing things. Something that was already "dead." Fanucci represents the gentile old ways coming face to face with the young and vicious Vito.

- **Michael and Death sitting in a tree, K-I-L-L-I-N-G—**Michael's bodyguard in *Godfather II* is clothed completely in black and says absolutely nothing for an entire movie. He hovers over Michael's shoulder and, except for a nod or two, never once does Michael speak to or look at him. It's like he's not even there in the same room with Michael, even when they are only a few feet apart. He's the angel or specter of Death, like a character from an Ingomar Bergman film, and he is watching over Mike. He protects him. Why? Because Michael is one of his best suppliers. So they see Havana together, with Death taking a bit of a holiday. The only time Michael looks at him is when he silently gives the order to kill Hyman. Symbolically, Michael turns his back on Hyman and turns toward his older pal, Death, for a bailout.

- **Mary Corleone is Mary for a reason**—She's virtuous, she's innocent, and she's *innocent. Unsullied.* A virgin. With her death at the opera, there died the last thing good about Michael. Michael's silent operatic scream of anguish was like his soul leaving his body. Minutes later in the movie, the already-dead Michael keels over and hits the ground, his first stop downward on his journey to Hell.

- **Speaking of innocent..Apollonia**—She was named Apollonia for a reason. It's because Apollo was the god of healing. In falling in love with her, Michael was healing himself, cleansing himself of his violent past. Of course, how'd that work out for him?

- **Woltz's temper tantrum in *Godfather I***—Tom and Mr. Woltz are having a nice dinner and chat.

Then Woltz goes crazy, screaming he's going to run Johnny Fontaine out of the business because he was made to look ridiculous when Johnny ran off with the starlet. There's no iconography here, but the point is made about the contrasting styles of the Corleones, versus Woltz. Woltz is driven by ego or "the personal"; Vito is driven by "business."

- **Fish sleepovers**—The murder of Luca Brassi was punctuated with the Sicilian message, "he sleeps with the fishes." Fredo himself was murdered years later while.. fishing. I wonder what kind of message a fish sends when he kills another fish? "Flounder sleeps with us."

- **Hyman Roth's birthday cake**—A picture of Cuba, being sliced up by the captains of American industry. Did you notice that Hyman's age is on the cake? Hyman was sixty-seven at the time and, quite frankly, looked terrible. But two generations ago, when someone turned sixty-five, they started thinking about death. Now they start thinking about taking Pilates.

- **Havana, New Year's Eve**—Take a look at the joyless, conversation-less partygoers. The attendees here are already corpses/ghosts. Their lack of expression and life signifies that on this night, their way of life will die and they will fade away.

- **Fredo! That's why they call him Superman—** This one is a stretch, but here goes. I think it's significant that Fredo takes his entourage, Michael, and the captains of industry, out to the pornographic *Superman* show then raves about the spectacle of Superman's gear. It shows that Fredo himself is in awe of "supermen," like Michael, Vito, and Hyman, and yearns to be like them.

- **Michael's name**—Michael was Vito's great American hope. He was the one that Vito wanted to make it big as a successful American business-man, lawyer, doctor. It's significant that of the three sons, he's the only one with a purely Anglican American-type name, Michael or Mike, as opposed to Santino and Fredo.

- **Michael and Kay: Love American Style**—Kay was the all American girl from New Hampshire. Michael's marriage to her was a step toward American-style legitimacy. Though it wasn't ar-ticulated in the movies, Vito probably approved of the marriage and saw it as a good move for Michael in terms of distancing himself from his dirty past and in Americanizing future Corleone stock.

- **Saint Santino**—One of Sonny's first actions as act-ing Don is to order Paulie's execution. As Sonny/ Santino takes command, we see a crucifix hanging prominently around his neck. His name means "saint" (Santino). He's a saint who kills, representing the vengeful God. He's also a pre-destined martyr. In these scenes, Sonny appears to be up to the job. As the plots thicken, though, so does Sonny's skull.

- **Mike's broken jaw**—After McCluskey's colossal haymaker, Michael's face swells up into something grotesque and unrecognizable. Just as Mike's face is transforming into something twisted and ugly, so is his soul as he dives into crime with both feet. What would have happened if McCluskey had punched Mike in the stomach? We'll never know.

- **The execution of Paulie**—There is some interesting imagery going on here, but I don't honestly know what it means. When Paulie is shot, you see the Statue of Liberty in the background. Does this mean that we are a violent nation and this is how we do business? Clemenza urinates during the execution. It was a pretext to stop the car in the weeds, sure, but there must be something else going on. Clemenza is in the act of elimination as Paulie is eliminated. If I ever run into Mr. Coppola, which is unlikely, I will have to ask him about the scene. If I run into him in a men's room, it will be poetic.

- **Michael alone in the courtyard**—As Clemenza and the real men are huddled in the kitchen making sauce, Mike shuffles his feet like a bored little kid. Off to the right is a statue of a cherub at play. Compared to Clemenza and the other hard-boiled types, Mike is like a little cherub. A child. And he is starting to hate it.

- **I'm with you, Pop. I'm with you**—When Michael hides the wounded Vito in the hospital supply closet, he whispers, "I'm with you...." Mike has now crossed over and is letting Dad know he's joined the battle. Vito smiles and thinks, *That's nice, but you're pulling on my catheter tube.*

- **Mike lights Enzo's cigarette**—After their close call with the hit men outside the hospital, Enzo the baker tries to light a cigarette. His hands are shaking too badly. Mike lights it for him then looks at his own hand. He's not shaking at all. Mike is starting to realize he's a natural for this kind of work.

- **Mike and Sonny and their women**—In consecutive scenes, we see Michael walking in Sicily with the virtuous Apollonia, under the supervision of the women of Corleone, and keeping his hands to himself. In the next scene, we see Sonny emerging from an afternoon quickie with his mistress. Virtue from the virtuous guy. Slutty-ness from the bad boy. Guess who's going to survive to see *Godfather II*?

* * *

Made in the USA
Lexington, KY
25 November 2010